Course	Writing Level 2
Course Number	**ESOL 0052**

Ronda Glasser
Cathy McDade

RICHLAND COLLEGE

WORLD LANGUAGES & CULTURES
AECI

http://create.mheducation.com

ISBN-10: 1308285833   ISBN-13: 9781308285832

Contents

Credits

CHAPTER

3

Four Steps for Writing, Four Bases for Revising

CHAPTER PREVIEW

What Are the Steps to Writing Effective Paragraphs?

- Step 1: Make a Point
- Step 2: Back Up Your Point
- Step 3: Organize the Support
- Step 4: Write Clear, Error-Free Sentences

Four Bases for Revising Writing

- Base 1: Unity
- Base 2: Support
- Base 3: Coherence
- Base 4: Sentence Skills

RESPONDING TO IMAGES

Has anyone misunderstood something you wrote? What happened? What did you write to make that person get the wrong idea? Take a few minutes to recount your experience. In this chapter, you'll learn how to write clearly so that others don't misinterpret your point.

What Are the Steps to Writing Effective Paragraphs?

To write an effective paragraph, you should begin by making a point, and then go on to support that point with specific evidence. Finally, end your paper with a sentence that rounds off the paragraph and provides a sense of completion.

Step 1: Make a Point

It is often best to state your point in the first sentence of your paragraph, as Mike does in his paragraph about working at a diner and truck stop. The sentence that expresses the main idea, or point, of a paragraph is called the *topic sentence*. Your paragraph will be unified if you make sure that all the details support the point in your topic sentence.

It is helpful to remember that a topic sentence is a *general* statement. The sentences that follow it provide specific support for the general statement.

Understanding the Paragraph	ACTIVITY 1

Each group of sentences in the following activity could be written as a short paragraph. Circle the letter of the topic sentence in each case. To find the topic sentence, ask yourself, "Which is a general statement supported by the specific details in the other three statements?"

Begin by trying the following example item. First circle the letter of the sentence you think expresses the main idea. Then read the explanation.

EXAMPLE

    a. CNN.com provides market trading information.

    b. CNN.com is a good source of national and world news.

    c. CNN.com has a lot to offer its readers.

    d. There are many video clips and podcasts available on CNN.com.

> **EXPLANATION:** Sentence *a* explains one important benefit of CNN.com. Sentences *b* and *d* provide other specific advantages of CNN.com. In sentence *c*, however, no one specific benefit is explained. Instead, the words "a lot to offer" refer only generally to such benefits. Therefore, sentence *c* is the topic sentence; it expresses the main idea. The other sentences support that idea by providing examples.

1.   a. Food and toiletries can be purchased at bulk prices.

    b. The price of gasoline is cheaper at a warehouse club.

    c. My family and I enjoy shopping at warehouse clubs.

    d. My children love the food samples.

2. a. Instead of talking on the telephone, we send text messages.
   b. People rarely talk to one another these days.
   c. Rather than talking with family members, we sit silently in front of the TV or computer all evening.
   d. In cars, we ignore our traveling companions to listen to the radio.

3. a. Once I completely forgot to study for a history final.
   b. During finals week, something awful always happens.
   c. The city bus was twenty minutes late on the day of my English final.
   d. Another time, the battery in my calculator died during my math final.

4. a. Today's retail environment relies on a variety of technologies.
   b. Cash registers operate on point-of-sale software.
   c. Merchandise is tracked through hand-held barcode scanners.
   d. Anti-shoplifting devices help reduce retail theft.

5. a. The submission techniques in MMA were developed from jujitsu and judo.
   b. Mixed martial arts (MMA) is an evolution of different fighting techniques.
   c. Kickboxing and karate provided MMA with striking techniques.
   d. The clinching techniques in MMA were taken from wrestling and sumo.

Understanding the Topic Sentence

An effective topic sentence does two things. First, it presents the topic of the paragraph. Second, it expresses the writer's attitude or opinion or idea about the topic. For example, look at the following topic sentence:

Professional athletes are overpaid.

In the topic sentence, the topic is *professional athletes;* the writer's idea about the topic is that professional athletes *are overpaid.*

ACTIVITY 2	Topic Sentences

For each topic sentence that follows, underline the topic and double-underline the point of view that the writer takes toward the topic.

EXAMPLES

Living in a small town has many advantages.

Cell phones should be banned in schools.

1. The apartments on Walnut Avenue are a fire hazard.

2. Losing my job turned out to have benefits.

3. Blues is the most interesting form of American music.

4. Our neighbor's backyard is a dangerous place.

5. Paula and Jeff are a stingy couple.

6. Snakes do not deserve their bad reputation.

7. Pollution causes many problems in American cities.

8. New fathers should receive at least two weeks of "paternity leave."

9. People with low self-esteem often need to criticize others.

10. Learning to write effectively is largely a matter of practice.

Identifying Topics, Topic Sentences, and Support

The following activity will sharpen your sense of the differences between topics, topic sentences, and supporting sentences.

Breaking Down the Parts of a Paragraph	**ACTIVITY 3**

Each group of items below includes one topic, one main idea (expressed in a topic sentence), and two supporting details for that idea. In the space provided, label each item with one of the following:

> **T**   topic
> **MI**   main idea
> **SD**   supporting details

1. _____ a. The weather in the summer is often hot and sticky.

   _____ b. Summer can be an unpleasant time of year.

   _____ c. Summer.

   _____ d. Bug bites, poison ivy, and allergies are a big part of summertime.

2. _____ a. The new Ultimate sports car is bound to be very popular.

   _____ b. The company has promised to provide any repairs needed during the first three years at no charge.

   _____ c. Because it gets thirty miles per gallon of gas, it offers real savings on fuel costs.

   _____ d. The new Ultimate sports car.

3. _____ a. Decorating an apartment doesn't need to be expensive.

   _____ b. A few plants add a touch of color without costing a lot of money.

   _____ c. Inexpensive braided rugs can be bought to match nearly any furniture.

   _____ d. Decorating an apartment.

4. _____ a. Long practice sessions and busy game schedules take too much time away from schoolwork.

   _____ b. High school sports.

   _____ c. The competition between schools may become so intense that, depending on the outcome of one game, athletes are either adored or scorned.

   _____ d. High school sports put too much pressure on young athletes.

5. _____ a. After mapping out the best route to your destination, phone ahead for motel reservations.

   _____ b. A long car trip.

   _____ c. Following a few guidelines before a long car trip can help you avoid potential problems.

   _____ d. Have your car's engine tuned as well, and have the tires, brakes, and exhaust system inspected.

Step 2: Back Up Your Point

To support your point, you need to provide specific reasons, examples, and other details that explain and develop it. The more precise and particular your supporting details are, the better your readers can "see," "hear," and "feel" them.

Understanding General versus Specific Ideas

A paragraph is made up of a main idea, which is general, and the specific ideas that support it. So to write well, you must understand the difference between general and specific ideas.

It is helpful to realize that you use general and specific ideas all the time in your everyday life. For example, in choosing a film to rent, you may think, "Which should I rent, an action movie, a comedy, or a romance?" In such a case, *film* is the general idea, and *action movie, comedy*, and *romance* are the specific ideas.

Or you may decide to begin an exercise program. In that case, you might consider walking, pilates, or lifting weights. In this case, *exercise* is the general idea, and *walking, pilates*, and *lifting weights* are the specific ideas.

Or if you are talking to a friend about a date that didn't work out well, you may say, "The dinner was terrible, the car broke down, and we had little to say to each other." In this case, the general idea is *the date didn't work out well*, and the specific ideas are the three reasons you named.

The following activities will give you experience in recognizing the relationship between general and specific. They will also provide a helpful background for the information and additional activities that follow.

CHAPTER 3   Four Steps for Writing, Four Bases for Revising   51

Identifying General Ideas   ACTIVITY 4

Each group of words consists of one general idea and four specific ideas. The general idea includes all the specific ideas. Underline the general idea in each group.

EXAMPLE

subway bus train <u>public transportation</u> railway

1. raspy high-pitched voice deep screechy

2. breakfast food scrambled eggs Belgian waffles smoked bacon orange juice

3. Mars Venus planet Saturn Earth

4. pill syrup caplet tablet pain reliever

5. zoology botany chemistry science biology

6. surfing kayaking water sports rafting waterskiing

7. peony flower rose daisy tulip

8. Indian Pacific Atlantic ocean Mediterranean

9. ceremony wedding funeral graduation baptism

10. yup yeah yes yep yesh

Developing Specific Ideas   ACTIVITY 5

In each item below, one idea is general and the others are specific. The general idea includes the specific ones. In the spaces provided, write in two more specific ideas that are covered by the general idea.

EXAMPLE

General: exercises

Specific: chin-ups, jumping jacks, <u>sit-ups</u> , <u>push-ups</u>

> HINT   Refer to the images in the margins when answering item 5.

1. *General:* pizza toppings

   Specific: sausage, mushrooms, _____ , _____

2. *General:* furniture

   Specific: rocking chair, coffee table, _____ , _____

3. *General:* magazines

   Specific: Reader's Digest, Newsweek, _____ , _____

52   PART 2   Writing Effective Paragraphs

4. *General:* birds

   Specific: eagle, pigeon, _____ , _____

5. *General:* music

   Specific: classical, jazz, _____ , _____

6. *General:* cold symptoms

   Specific: aching muscles, watery eyes, _____ , _____

7. *General:* children's games

   Specific: hopscotch, dodgeball, _____ , _____

8. *General:* transportation

   Specific: plane, motorcycle, _____ , _____

9. *General:* city problems

   Specific: overcrowding, pollution, _____ , _____

10. *General:* types of TV shows

    Specific: cartoons, reality shows, _____ , _____

ACTIVITY 6   **What Ideas Have in Common**

Read each group of specific ideas below. Then circle the letter of the general idea that tells what the specific ideas have in common. Note that the general idea should not be too broad or too narrow. Begin by trying the example item, and then read the explanation that follows.

EXAMPLE

Specific ideas: peeling potatoes, washing dishes, cracking eggs, cleaning out refrigerator

The general idea is

a. household jobs.

b. kitchen tasks.

c. steps in making dinner.

> **EXPLANATION:** It is true that the specific ideas are all household jobs, but they have in common something even more specific—they are all tasks done in the kitchen. Therefore, answer *a* is too broad, and the correct answer is *b*. Answer *c* is too narrow because it doesn't cover all the specific ideas. Although two of them could be steps in making a dinner ("peeling potatoes" and "cracking eggs"), two have nothing to do with making dinner.

1. *Specific ideas:* crowded office, rude coworkers, demanding boss, unreasonable deadlines

   The general idea is

   a. problems.
   b. work problems.
   c. problems with work schedules.

2. *Specific ideas:* cactus, rosebush, fern, daisy

   The general idea is

   a. plants.
   b. plants that have thorns.
   c. plants that grow in the desert.

3. *Specific ideas:* Band-Aids, gauze, antiseptic, aspirin

   The general idea is

   a. supplies.
   b. first-aid supplies.
   c. supplies for treating a headache.

4. *Specific ideas:* trout, whales, salmon, frogs

   The general idea is

   a. animals.
   b. fish.
   c. animals living in water.

5. *Specific ideas:* Hershey bar, lollipop, mints, fudge

   The general idea is

   a. food.
   b. candy.
   c. chocolate.

6. *Specific ideas:* "Go to bed," "Pick up that trash," "Run twenty laps," "Type this letter."

   The general idea is

   a. remarks.
   b. orders.
   c. the boss's orders.

7. *Specific ideas:* "I had no time to study," "The questions were unfair," "I had a headache," "The instructor didn't give us enough time."

   The general idea is

   a. statements.
   b. excuses for being late.
   c. excuses for not doing well on a test.

54   PART 2   Writing Effective Paragraphs

8. *Specific ideas:* candle, sun, headlight, flashlight

   The general idea is

   a. things that are very hot.
   b. light sources for a home.
   c. sources of light.

9. *Specific ideas:* driving with expired license plates, driving over the speed limit, parking without putting money in the meter, driving without a license

   The general idea is:

   a. ways to cause a traffic accident.
   b. traffic problems.
   c. ways to get a ticket.

10. *Specific ideas:* "Are we there yet?" "Where do people come from?" "Can I have that toy?" "Do I have to go to bed now?"

    The general idea is

    a. Things adults say to one another.
    b. Things children ask adults.
    c. Things children ask at school.

ACTIVITY 7	What Is the General Idea?

In the following items, the specific ideas are given but the general ideas are unstated. Fill in the blanks with the general ideas.

EXAMPLE

General idea: _____ car problems _____

Specific ideas: flat tire   dented bumper
                    cracked windshield   dirty oil filter

1. *General idea:* _____

   Specific ideas: nephew   grandmother
                       aunt   cousin

2. *General idea:* _____

   Specific ideas: boots   sneakers
                       sandals   slippers

3. *General idea:* _____

   Specific ideas: camping   hiking
                       fishing   hunting

4. *General idea:* _____

   Specific ideas: broom   sponge
                       mop   glass cleaner

5. *General idea:* _____

   Specific ideas: cloudy   sunny
                        snowy   rainy

6. *General idea:* _____

   Specific ideas: Spread mustard on slice of bread
                        Add turkey and cheese
                        Put lettuce on top of cheese
                        Cover with another slice of bread

7. *General idea:* _____

   Specific ideas: thermos of lemonade   insect repellent
                        basket of food   blanket

8. *General idea:* _____

   Specific ideas: fleas in carpeting   loud barking
                        tangled fur   veterinary bills

9. *General idea:* _____

   Specific ideas: diabetes   cancer
                        appendicitis   broken leg

10. *General idea:* _____

    Specific ideas: flooded basements   wet streets
                         rainbow   overflowing rivers

Recognizing Specific Details

Specific details are examples, reasons, particulars, and facts. Such details are needed to support and explain a topic sentence effectively. They provide the evidence needed for us to understand, as well as to feel and experience, a writer's point.

Below is a topic sentence followed by two sets of supporting sentences. Write a check mark next to the set that provides sharp, specific details.

Topic sentence: **Ticket sales for a recent Rolling Stones concert proved that the classic rock band is still very popular.**

_____ a. Fans came from everywhere to buy tickets to the concert. People wanted good seats and were willing to endure a great deal of various kinds of discomfort as they waited in line for many hours. Some people actually waited for days, sleeping at night in uncomfortable circumstances. Good tickets were sold out extremely quickly

_____ b. The first person in the long ticket line spent three days standing in the hot sun and three nights sleeping on the concrete without even a pillow. The man behind her waited equally long in his wheelchair. The ticket window opened at 10:00 A.M., and the tickets for the good seats—those in front of the stage—were sold out an hour later.

56 PART 2 Writing Effective Paragraphs

> EXPLANATION: The second set (*b*) provides specific details. Instead of a vague statement about fans who were "willing to endure a great deal of various kinds of discomfort," we get vivid details we can see and picture clearly: "three days standing in the hot sun," "three nights sleeping on the concrete without even a pillow," and "The man behind her waited equally long in his wheelchair."
>
> Instead of a vague statement that tickets were "sold out extremely quickly," we get exact and vivid details: "The ticket window opened at 10:00 A.M., and the tickets for the good seats—those in front of the stage—were sold out an hour later."

Specific details are often like a movie script. They provide us with such clear pictures that we could make a film of them if we wanted to. You would know just how to film the information given in the second set of sentences. You would show the fans in line under a hot sun and, later, sleeping on the concrete. The first person in line would be shown sleeping without a pillow under her head. You would show tickets finally going on sale, and after an hour you could show the ticket seller explaining that all of the seats in front of the stage were sold out.

In contrast, the writer of the first set of sentences (*a*) fails to provide the specific information needed. If you were asked to make a film based on set *a*, you would have to figure out on your own just what particulars to show.

When you are working to provide specific supporting information in a paper, it might help to ask yourself, "Could someone easily film this information?" If the answer is yes, your supporting details are specific enough for your readers to visualize.

ACTIVITY 8	Specific vs. General Support

Each topic sentence in this activity is followed by two sets of supporting details. Write S (for *specific*) in the space next to the set that provides specific support for the point. Write G (for *general*) next to the set that offers only vague general support.

1. *Topic sentence:* Alonzo was relieved when he received the results from his physical exam.

    _____ a. Alonzo's blood pressure was 120/80, which is within the normal range for men. His cholesterol ratio was below 4, which is good for men of his age.

    _____ b. Alonzo's doctor told him that his blood pressure was normal. He also learned that his cholesterol levels were normal.

2. *Topic sentence:* When preparing meals on a budget, canned meats and beans provide cost-effective alternatives.

   _____ a. Canned meat can be used rather than fresh meat to prepare meals. Canned fish can also be used. Canned beans are another alternative when preparing economical meals.

   _____ b. Spam can be used instead of sirloin beef to prepare stews and stir-fry dishes. Canned tuna can be used to make baked casseroles and pasta meals. Canned kidney, pinto, and black beans can be used instead of ground beef to make chili and grilled burgers.

3. *Topic sentence:* My college campus provides students with valuable resources.

   _____ a. The writing tutors at the Learning Center help students find topics and assist them with revision and editing. The reference librarians at the library help students locate appropriate books and online journals for their research papers. The academic advisers at the Counseling Office notify students about required and elective courses during registration.

   _____ b. Tutors on campus help students with the different stages of their writing. Librarians help students with their research by locating different sources in the library and online. Counselors on campus provide students with useful information on course registration.

4. *Topic sentence:* RateMyProfessor.com provides students with a reliable source of information for finding out information about their professors.

   _____ a. On RateMyProfessor.com, students evaluate their professors. Professors are scored on their quality of teaching. They are also rated in other areas. The most helpful section of a rating is the user comments.

   _____ b. On RateMyProfessor.com, students give their professors a "scorecard." Professors are scored on their quality of teaching under the categories "good," "average," and "poor." They are also rated in terms of "easiness," "clarity," and "helpfulness." Some teachers are even awarded a "hot" chili pepper rating. The user comments—the most helpful section of the Web site—allows students to write honestly about what they liked and disliked about their professors.

5. *Topic sentence:* Employers are providing different work options to help employees reduce the cost of commuting to and from work.

   _____ a. Some employers are allowing their employees to work from home one day a week. Some employers are providing a condensed work week. Some employers are encouraging transportation alternatives and providing public transit incentives.

58 PART 2 Writing Effective Paragraphs

_____ b. Some employers are allowing employees to telecommute one day a week by using their home computer, the Internet, and phone and video conferencing. Some employers are condensing the work week from five eight-hour days to four ten-hour days. Some employers are encouraging employees to car pool, and they are paying for monthly bus and rail passes.

ACTIVITY 9	Specific vs. General Support in a Paragraph

At several points in each of the following paragraphs, you are given a choice of two sets of supporting details. Write _S_ (for _specific_) in the space next to the set that provides specific support for the point. Write _G_ (for _general_) next to the set that offers only vague, general support.

PARAGRAPH 1

My daughter is as shy as I am, and it breaks my heart to see her dealing with the same problems I had to deal with in my childhood because of my shyness. I feel very sad for her when I see the problems she has making friends.

_____ a. It takes her a long time to begin to do the things other children do to make friends, and her feelings get hurt very easily over one thing or another. She is not at all comfortable about making connections with her classmates at school.

_____ b. She usually spends Christmas vacation alone because by that time of year she doesn't have friends yet. Only when her birthday comes in the summer is she confident enough to invite school friends to her party. Once she sends out the invitations, she almost sleeps by the telephone, waiting for the children to respond. If they say they can't come, her eyes fill with tears.

I recognize very well her signs of shyness, which make her look smaller and more fragile than she really is.

_____ c. When she has to talk to someone she doesn't know well, she speaks in a whisper and stares sideways. Pressing her hands together, she lifts her shoulders as though she wished she could hide her head between them.

_____ d. When she is forced to talk to anyone other than her family and her closest friends, the sound of her voice and the position of her head change. Even her posture changes in a way that makes it look as if she's trying to make her body disappear.

It is hard for me to watch her passing unnoticed at school.

_____ e. She never gets chosen for a special job or privilege, even though she tries her best, practicing in privacy at home. She just doesn't measure up. Worst of all, even her teacher seems to forget her existence much of the time.

_____ f. Although she rehearses in our basement, she never gets chosen for a good part in a play. Her voice is never loud or clear enough. Worst of all, her teacher doesn't call on her in class for days at a time.

PARAGRAPH 2

It is said that the dog is man's best friend, but I strongly believe that the honor belongs to my computer. A computer won't fetch a stick for me, but it can help me entertain myself in many ways.

_____ a. If I am bored, tired, or out of ideas, the computer allows me to explore things that interest me, such as anything relating to the world of professional sports.

_____ b. The other day, I used my computer to visit the National Football League's Web site. I was then able to get injury updates for players on my favorite team, the Philadelphia Eagles.

While the dog is a faithful friend, it does not allow me to be a more responsible person the way my computer does.

_____ c. I use my computer to pay all my bills online. I also use it to balance my checkbook and keep track of my expenses. Now I always know how much money is in my account at the end of the month.

_____ d. The computer helps me be responsible with financial matters because it records my transactions. With the computer, I have access to more information, which allows me to make good decisions with my money.

A dog might help me meet strangers I see in the park, but the computer helps me meet people who share my interests.

_____ e. With my computer, I can go online and find people with every type of hobby or interest. Thousands of blogs and discussion groups are available featuring people from all over the country—and the world. The computer can even allow me to develop meaningful personal relationships with others.

_____ f. Two months ago, I discovered a Web site for people in my community who enjoy hiking. I'm planning to meet a group next Saturday for a day hike. And earlier this year, I met my wonderful fiancée, Shelly, through an online dating service.

60   PART 2   Writing Effective Paragraphs

Providing Specific Details

ACTIVITY 10	Getting Specific

Each of the following sentences contains a general word or words, set off in *italic* type. Substitute sharp, specific words in each case.

EXAMPLE

After the parade, the city street was littered with *garbage*.

After the parade, the city street was littered with multicolored confetti, dirty popcorn, and lifeless balloons.

1. If I had enough money, I'd visit *several places*.

2. It took her *a long time* to get home.

3. Ron is often stared at because of his *unusual hair color and hairstyle*.

4. After you pass *two buildings*, you'll see my house on the left.

5. Nia's purse is crammed with *lots of stuff*.

6. I bought *some junk food* for the long car trip.

7. The floor in the front of my car is covered with *things*.

8. When his mother said no to his request for a toy, the child *reacted strongly*.

9. Devan gave his girlfriend a *surprise present* for Valentine's Day.

_____

_____

10. My cat can *do a wonderful trick.*

_____

_____

Selecting Details That Fit

The details in your paper must all clearly relate to and support your opening point. If a detail does not support your point, leave it out. Otherwise, your paper will lack unity. For example, see if you can circle the letter of the two sentences that do *not* support the following topic sentence.

Topic sentence: **Tom is a very talented person.**

a. Tom is always courteous to his professors.
b. He has created beautiful paintings in his art course.
c. Tom is the lead singer in a local band.
d. He won an award in a photography contest.
e. He is hoping to become a professional photographer.

> **EXPLANATION:** Being courteous may be a virtue, but it is not a talent, so sentence *a* does not support the topic sentence. Also, Tom's desire to become a professional photographer tells us nothing about his talent; thus, sentence *e* does not support the topic sentence either. The other three statements all clearly back up the topic sentence. Each in some way supports the idea that Tom is talented—in art, as a singer, or as a photographer.

Details That Don't Fit	ACTIVITY 11

In each group below, circle the two items that do *not* support the topic sentence.

1. *Topic sentence:* Carla seems attracted only to men who are unavailable.
    a. She once fell in love with a man serving a life sentence in prison.
    b. Her parents worry about her inability to connect with a nice single man.
    c. She wants to get married and have kids before she is thirty.
    d. Her current boyfriend is married.
    e. Recently she had a huge crush on a Catholic priest.

2. *Topic sentence:* Some dog owners have little consideration for other people.

   a. Obedience lessons can be a good experience for both the dog and the owner.

   b. Some dog owners let their dogs leave droppings on the sidewalk or in other people's yards.

   c. They leave the dog home alone for hours, and it barks and howls and wakes the neighbors.

   d. Some people keep very large dogs in small apartments.

   e. Even when small children are playing nearby, owners let their bad-tempered dogs run loose.

3. *Topic sentence:* Dr. Eliot is a very poor teacher.

   a. He cancels class frequently with no explanation.

   b. When a student asks a question that he can't answer, he becomes irritated with the student.

   c. He got his PhD at a university in another country.

   d. He's taught at the college for many years and is on a number of faculty committees.

   e. He puts off grading papers until the end of the semester, and then returns them all at once.

4. *Topic sentence:* Some doctors seem to think it is all right to keep patients waiting.

   a. Pharmaceutical sales representatives sometimes must wait hours to see a doctor.

   b. The doctors stand in the hallway chatting with nurses and secretaries even when they have a waiting room full of patients.

   c. Patients sometimes travel long distances to consult with a particular doctor.

   d. When a patient calls before an appointment to see if the doctor is on time, the answer is often yes even when the doctor is two hours behind schedule.

   e. Some doctors schedule appointments in a way that ensures long lines, to make it appear that they are especially skillful.

5. *Topic sentence:* Several factors were responsible for the staggering loss of lives when the *Titanic* sank.

   a. More than 1,500 people died in the *Titanic* disaster; only 711 survived.

   b. Despite warnings about the presence of icebergs, the captain allowed the *Titanic* to continue at high speed.

   c. If the ship had hit the iceberg head-on, its watertight compartments might have kept it from sinking; however, it hit on the side, resulting in a long, jagged gash through which water poured in.

   d. The *Titanic*, equipped with the very best communication systems available in 1912, sent out SOS messages.

   e. When the captain gave orders to abandon the *Titanic*, many passengers refused because they believed the ship was unsinkable, so many lifeboats were only partly filled.

Providing Details That Fit

Writing Specific Details   ACTIVITY 12

Each topic sentence in this activity is followed by one supporting detail. See if you can add a second detail in each case. Make sure your detail supports the topic sentence.

1. *Topic sentence:* There are valid reasons why students miss deadlines.

   a. Students may have more than one paper to write on any given day.

   b. _____

2. *Topic sentence:* Those who serve in the military make many sacrifices.

   a. They leave their families to serve on tours of duty.

   b. _____

3. *Topic sentence:* Sabrina has such a positive outlook on life.

   a. When she lost her job, she contacted an employment agency right away.

   b. _____

4. *Topic sentence:* There are many advantages to group work.

   a. Everyone has talents to contribute.

   b. _____

5. *Topic sentence:* Everyone should take measures to prevent identity theft.

   a. Passwords should be changed regularly.

   b. _____

Providing Support   ACTIVITY 13

Working in pairs, see if you can add *two* supporting details for each of the following topic sentences.

1. *Topic sentence:* The managers of this apartment building don't care about their renters.

   a. Mrs. Harris has been asking them to fix her leaky faucet for two months.

   b. _____

   c. _____

2. *Topic sentence:* None of the shirts for sale were satisfactory.

   a. Some were attractive but too expensive.

   b. _____

   c. _____

64   PART 2   Writing Effective Paragraphs

3. *Topic sentence:* After being married for forty years, Mr. and Mrs. Lambert have grown similar in odd ways.

   a. They both love to have a cup of warm apple juice just before bed.

   b. _____

   c. _____

4. *Topic sentence:* It is a special time for me when my brother is in town.

   a. We always catch the latest sci-fi thriller and then stop for pizza.

   b. _____

   c. _____

5. *Topic sentence:* Our neighbor's daughter is very spoiled.

   a. When anyone else in the family has a birthday, she gets several presents too.

   b. _____

   c. _____

Providing Details in a Paragraph

ACTIVITY 14	Adding Details to a Paragraph

The following paragraph needs specific details to back up its three supporting points. In the spaces provided, write two or three sentences of convincing details for each supporting point.

A Disappointing Concert

Although I had looked forward to seeing my favorite band in concert, the experience was disappointing. For one thing, our seats were terrible, in two ways. _____

_____

_____

In addition, the crowd made it hard to enjoy the music. _____

_____

_____

_____

continued

And finally, the band members acted as if they didn't want to be there. _____

_____

_____

_____

Omitting and Grouping Details in Planning a Paragraph

One common way to develop material for a paper involves three steps: (1) Make a list of details about your point, (2) omit details that don't truly support your point, and (3) group remaining details together in logical ways. Omitting details that don't fit and grouping related details together are part of learning how to write effectively.

Grouping Details   ACTIVITY 15

See if you can figure out a way to put the following details into three groups. Write *A* in front of the details that go with one group, *B* in front of the details that go with a second group, and *C* in front of the details that make up a third group. Cross out the four details that do not relate to the topic sentence.

Topic sentence: My brother Sean caused our parents lots of headaches when he was a teenager.

_____ In constant trouble at school

_____ While playing a joke on his lab partner, nearly blew up the chemistry lab

_____ Girlfriend was eight years older than he and had been married twice

_____ Girlfriend had a very sweet four-year-old son

_____ Parents worried about people Sean spent his time with

_____ Several signs that he was using drugs

_____ Failed so many courses that he had to go to summer school in order to graduate

_____ Was suspended twice for getting into fights between classes

_____ Our father taught math at the high school we attended

_____ His money just disappeared, and he never had anything to show for it

_____ His best pal had been arrested for armed robbery

66   PART 2   Writing Effective Paragraphs

———— Often looked glassy-eyed

———— Hung around with older kids who had dropped out of school

———— Until he was in eighth grade, he had always been on the honor roll

———— No one was allowed in his room, which he kept locked whenever he was away from home

———— Has managed to turn his life around now that he's in college

> EXPLANATION: After thinking about the list for a while, you probably real-ized that the details about Sean's trouble at school form one group. He got in trouble at school for nearly blowing up the chemistry lab, failing courses, and fighting between classes. Another group of details has to do with his parents' worrying about the people he spent time with. His parents were worried because he had an older girlfriend, a best friend who was arrested for armed robbery, and older friends who were school dropouts. Finally, there are the details about signs that he was using drugs: his money disappearing, his glassy-eyed appearance, and not allowing others in his room.
>
> The main idea—that as a teenager, the writer's brother caused their parents lots of headaches—can be supported with three kinds of evidence: the trouble he got into at school, his friends, and the signs indicating he was on drugs. The other four items in the list do not logically go with any of these three types of evidence and so should be omitted.

ACTIVITY 16   Omitting and Grouping Details

This activity will give you practice in omitting and grouping details. See if you can figure out a way to put the following details into three groups. Write *A* in front of the details that go with one group, *B* in front of the details that go with a second group, and *C* in front of the details that make up a third group. Cross out the four details that do not relate to the topic sentence.

Topic sentence: There are practical ways for college students to manage their time wisely.

———— Students should guard how they spend their time.

———— Students should keep track of how they spend their time.

———— College students also have a difficult time managing their money.

———— A time log will tell them how much time they spend study-ing, working, and so forth.

———— They should avoid distractions—the TV, the Internet, the phone, for example—when studying.

———— Students should prioritize how they spend their time.

_____ A monthly calendar will allow them to record important due dates and appointments.

_____ A time log will tell them how much time they waste and how they waste it.

_____ Parents need to manage their time wisely.

_____ Students miss deadlines because they are unable to manage their time.

_____ They should ask their family members and friends to respect their regular study time.

_____ A daily to-do list will allow them to prioritize what needs to be accomplished.

_____ Some students even fail classes because of their poor time-management skills.

_____ They should talk to their employer if their work schedule conflicts with their study time.

_____ A time log can provide information on whether students are managing their time wisely.

_____ Calendars and to-do lists are specific tools that students can use to prioritize their time.

Step 3: Organize the Support

You will find it helpful to learn two common ways of organizing support in a paragraph—*listing order* and *time order.* You should also learn the signal words, known as *transitions,* that increase the effectiveness of each method.

Transitions are words and phrases that indicate relationships between ideas. They are like signposts that guide travelers, showing them how to move smoothly from one spot to the next. Be sure to take advantage of transitions. They will help organize and connect your ideas, and they will help your readers follow the direction of your thoughts.

Listing Order

A writer can organize supporting evidence in a paper by providing a list of two or more reasons, examples, or details. Often the most important or interesting item is saved for last because the reader is most likely to remember the last thing read.

Transition words that indicate listing order include the following:

one	second	also	next	last of all
for one thing	third	another	moreover	finally
first of all	next	in addition	furthermore	

68   PART 2   Writing Effective Paragraphs

Mike's paragraph about working at the diner and truck stop (Chapter 1, p. 8) uses listing order: It lists three reasons why it was the worst job he ever had, and each of those three reasons is introduced by one of the preceding transitions. In the following spaces, write in the three transitions:

___First of all___   ___Second___   ___Finally___

The first reason in the paragraph about working at the plant is introduced with *first of all*, the second reason by *second,* and the third reason by *finally.*

| ACTIVITY 17 | **Using Listing Order** |

Use *listing order* to arrange the scrambled list of sentences below. Number each supporting sentence 1, 2, 3, . . . so that you go from the least important item to what is presented as the most important item.

Note that transitions will help by making clear the relationships between some of the sentences.

Topic sentence: I am no longer a big fan of professional sports, for a number of reasons.

_____ Basketball and hockey continue well into the baseball season, and football doesn't have its Super Bowl until the middle of winter, when basketball should be at center stage.

_____ In addition, I detest the high fives, taunting, and trash talk that so many professional athletes now indulge in during games.

_____ Second, I am bothered by the length of professional sports seasons.

_____ Also, professional athletes have no loyalty to a team or city, as they greedily sell their abilities to the highest bidder.

_____ For one thing, greed is the engine running professional sports.

_____ There are numerous news stories of professional athletes in trouble with the law because of drugs, guns, fights, traffic accidents, or domestic violence.

_____ After a good year, athletes making millions become unhappy if they aren't rewarded with a new contract calling for even more millions.

_____ But the main reason I've become disenchanted with professional sports is the disgusting behavior of so many of its athletes.

Time Order

When a writer uses time order, supporting details are presented in the order in which they occurred. *First* this happened; *next* this; *after* that, this; and so on. Many paragraphs, especially paragraphs that tell a story or give a series of directions, are organized in a time order.

Transition words that show time relationships include the following:

first	before	after	when	then
next	during	now	while	until
as	soon	later	often	finally

Read the following paragraph, which is organized in time order. See if you can underline the six transition words that show the time relationships.

> Della had a sad experience while driving home last night. She traveled along the dark, winding road that led toward her home. She was only two miles from her house when she noticed a glimmer of light in the road. The next thing she knew, she heard a sickening thud and realized she had struck an animal. The light, she realized, had been its eyes reflected in her car's headlights. Della stopped the car and ran back to see what she had hit. It was a handsome cocker spaniel, with blond fur and long ears. As she bent over the still form, she realized there was nothing to be done. The dog was dead. Della searched the dog for a collar and tags. There was nothing. Before leaving, she walked to several nearby houses, asking if anyone knew who owned the dog. No one did. Finally Della gave up and drove on. She was sad to leave someone's pet lying there alone.

The main point of the paragraph is stated in its first sentence: "Della had a sad experience while driving home last night." The support for this point is all the details of Della's experience. Those details are presented in the order in which they occurred. The time relationships are highlighted by these transitions: *while, when, next, as, before,* and *finally.*

Using Time Order	**ACTIVITY 18**

Use *time order* to arrange the scrambled sentences below. Number the supporting sentences in the order in which they occur in time (1, 2, 3, . . .).

Note that transitions will help by making clear the relationships between sentences.

Topic sentence: If people have difficulty sleeping, the following steps should help.

_____ Also, they should avoid taking naps during the daytime.

_____ They should start by getting up early to ensure their bodies are tired by the end of the day.

_____ During the evening, it is important to avoid drinking caffeine, which is a stimulant.

_____ Finally, they should go to bed at a reasonable and regular time each evening.

_____ During the daytime, they should fit regular exercise into their schedules.

_____ Before they go to bed, they should avoid reading.

_____ First, they should check with their doctors to rule out any medical problems such as sleep apnea.

_____ In addition, watching TV before bed should be avoided.

More about Using Transitions

As already stated, transitions are signal words that help readers follow the direction of the writer's thoughts. To see the value of transitions, look at the two versions of the short paragraph below. Check the version that is easier to read and understand.

_____ a. There are several sources that a student can use for writing assignments. Personal experience is a major resource. For an assignment about communication skills, for instance, a student can draw on personal experiences in college, at work, and in everyday life. Other people's experiences are extremely useful. A personal friend, colleague, boss, or even experts on TV who are knowledgeable about communication skills could be used as a resource. A student could interview people. Books, magazines, and the Internet are good sources of material for assignments. Many experts, for example, have written about various aspects of communication skills.

_____ b. There are several sources that a student can use for writing assignments. First of all, personal experience is a major resource. For an assignment about communication skills, for instance, a student can draw on personal experiences in college, at work, and in everyday life. In addition, other people's experiences are extremely useful. A personal friend, colleague, boss, or even people on TV who have talked about communication skills could be used as a resource. A student could also interview people. Finally, books, magazines, and the Internet are good sources of material for assignments. Many experts, for example, have written about various aspects of communication skills.

CHAPTER 3   Four Steps for Writing, Four Bases for Revising   71

> **EXPLANATION:**   You no doubt chose the second version, *b*. The listing transitions—*first of all, in addition,* and *finally*—make it clear when the author is introducing a new supporting point. The reader of paragraph *b* is better able to follow the author's line of thinking and to note that three main sources of material for assignments are being listed: your own experience, other people's experiences, and books, magazines, and the Internet.

Using Transitions   **ACTIVITY 19**

The following paragraphs use listing order or time order. In each case, fill in the blanks with appropriate transitions from the box above the paragraph. Use each transition once.

1.

after	now	first	soon	while

My husband has developed an involving hobby, in which I, unfortunately, am unable to share. He _____ enrolled in ground flight instruction classes at the local community college. The lessons were all about air safety regulations and procedures. _____ passing a difficult exam, he decided to take flying lessons at the city airport. Every Monday he would wake at six o'clock in the morning and drive happily to the airport, eager to see his instructor. _____ he was taking lessons, he started to buy airplane magazines and talk about them constantly. "Look at that Cessna 150," he would say. "Isn't she a beauty?" _____, after many lessons, he is flying by himself. _____ he will be able to carry passengers. That is my biggest nightmare. I know he will want me to fly with him, but I am not a lover of heights. I can't understand why someone would leave the safety of the ground to be in the sky, defenseless as a kite.

2.

finally	for one thing	second

The karate class I took last week convinced me that martial arts may never be my strong point. _____, there is the issue of balance. The instructor asked everyone in class to stand on one foot to practice kicking. Each time I tried, I wobbled and had to spread my arms out wide to avoid falling. I even stumbled into Mr. Kim, my instructor, who glared at me. _____, there was the issue of flexibility. Mr. Kim asked us to stretch and touch our toes. Everyone did this without a problem—except me. I could barely reach my knees before pain raced up and down my back. _____, there was my lack of coordination. When everyone started practicing blocks, I got confused. I couldn't figure out where to move my arms and legs. By the time I got the first move right, the whole group had finished three more. By the end of my first lesson, I was completely lost.

3.
later	soon	when	then

At the age of thirty-one I finally had the opportunity to see snow for the first time in my life. It was in New York City on a cloudy afternoon in November. My daughter and I had gone to the American Museum of Natural History. _____ we left the museum, snow was falling gently. I thought that it was so beautiful! It made me remember movies I had seen countless times in my native Brazil. We decided to find a taxi. _____ we were crossing Central Park, snuggled in the cozy cab, watching the snow cover trees, bushes, branches, and grass. We were amazed to see the landscape quickly change from fall to winter. _____ we arrived in front of our hotel, and I still remember stepping on the crisp snow and laughing like a child who is touched by magic. _____ that day, I heard on the radio that another snowstorm was coming. I was naive enough to wait for thunder and the other sounds of a rainstorm. I did not know yet that snow, even a snowstorm, is silent and soft.

4.
last of all	another	first of all	in addition

Public school students who expect to attend school from September to June, and then have a long summer vacation, may be in for a big surprise before long. For a number of reasons, many schools are switching to a year-round calendar. _____, many educators point out that the traditional school calendar was established years ago when young people had to be available during the summer months to work on farms, but this necessity has long since passed. _____ reason is that a longer school year accommodates individual learning rates more effectively—that is, fast learners can go into more depth about a subject that interests them, while those who learn at a slower pace have more time to master the essential material. _____, many communities have gone to year-round school to relieve overcrowding, since students can be put on different schedules throughout the year. _____, and perhaps most important, educators feel that year-round schools eliminate the loss of learning that many students experience over a long summer break.

Step 4: Write Clear, Error-Free Sentences

If you use correct spelling and follow the rules of grammar, punctuation, and usage, your sentences will be clear and well written. But by no means must you have all that information in your head. Even the best writers need to use reference materials to be sure their writing is correct. So when you write your papers, keep a good dictionary and grammar handbook nearby.

In general, however, save them for after you've gotten your ideas firmly down in writing. You'll find as you write paragraphs that you will make a number of sentence errors. Simply ignore them until you get to a later draft of your paper, when there will be time enough to make the needed corrections. Part 3 of this text focuses on sentence skills.

Four Bases for Revising Writing

In this chapter, you've learned four essential steps in writing an effective paragraph. The following box shows how these steps lead to four standards, or bases, you can use in evaluating and revising paragraphs.

Four Steps ➡	Four Bases
1. If you make one point and stick to that point,	➡ your writing will have *unity*.
2. If you back up the point with specific eveience,	➡ your writing will have *support*.
3. If you organize and connect the speficic evidence,	➡ your writing will have *coherence*.
4. If you write clear, error-free sentences,	➡ your writing will demonstrate effective *sentence skills*.

Base 1: Unity

Understanding Unity

To achieve unity is to have all the details in your paper related to the single point expressed in the topic sentence, the first sentence. Each time you think of something to put in, ask yourself whether it relates to your main point. If if does not, leave it out. For example, if you were writing about a certain job as the worst job you ever had and then spent a couple of sentences talking about the interesting people you met there, you would be missing the first and most essential base of good writing.

> **TIP** To check a paragraph for unity, ask yourself these questions:
> 1. Is there a clear, single point in the first sentence of the paragraph?
> 2. Is all the evidence on target in support of the opening point?

Evaluating a Paragraph for Unity

ACTIVITY 20	**Omitting Off-Target Sentences**

The following paragraph contains two sentences that are off target—sentences that do not support the opening point—and so the paragraph is not unified. In the interest of paragraph unity, such sentences must be omitted.

Cross out the off-target sentences and write the numbers of those sentences in the spaces provided.

How to Prevent Plagiarism

[1]Instructors should take steps to prevent students from cheating on exams. [2]To begin with, instructors should stop reusing old tests. [3]A test that has been used even once is soon known on the student grapevine. [4]Students will check with their friends to find out, for example, what was on Dr. Patel's biology final last term. [5]They may even manage to find a copy of the test itself, "accidentally" not turned in by a former student of Dr. Patel's. [6]Instructors should also take some commonsense precautions at test time. [7]They should make students separate themselves—at least by one seat—during an exam. [8]They should also ban cell phones during an exam. [9]If a student is found using a cell phone, that instructor should take it away. [10]Last of all, instructors must make it clear to students that there will be stiff penalties for cheating. [11]One of the problems with our school systems is a lack of discipline. [12]Instructors never used to give in to students' demands or put up with bad behavior, as they do today. [13]Anyone caught cheating should immediately receive a zero for the exam. [14]A person even suspected of cheating should be forced to take an alternative exam in the instructor's office. [15]Because cheating is unfair to honest students, it should not be tolerated.

The numbers of the off-target sentences: _____ _____

Base 2: Support

Understanding Support

The second base of effective writing, *support,* provides specific examples that illustrate the main point of a paragraph. Readers want to see and judge for ourselves whether a writer is making a valid point about a subject, but without specific details we cannot do so. After realizing the importance of specific supporting details, one student writer revised a paper she had done on a restaurant job as the worst job she ever had. In the revised paper, instead of talking about "unsanitary conditions in the kitchen," she referred to such specifics as "green mold on the bacon" and "ants in the potato salad." All your paragraphs should include many vivid details! Using ample support will help you communicate more clearly and effectively in your writing.

> **TIP** To check a paragraph for support, ask yourself these questions:
> 1. Is there *specific* evidence to support the opening point?
> 2. Is there *enough* specific evidence?

Evaluating Paragraphs for Support

Checking for Specific Details   ACTIVITY 21

The paragraph that follows lacks sufficient supporting details. Identify the spot or spots where more specific details are needed.

Culture Conflict

¹I am in a constant tug-of-war with my parents over conflicts between their Vietnamese culture and American culture. ²To begin with, my parents do not like me to have American friends. ³They think that I should spend all my time with other Vietnamese people and speak English only when necessary. ⁴I get into an argument whenever I want to go to a fast-food restaurant or a movie at night with my American friends. ⁵The conflict with my parents is even worse when it comes to plans for a career. ⁶My parents want me to get a degree in science and then go on to medical school. ⁷On the other hand, I think I want to become a teacher. ⁸So far I have been taking both science and education courses, but soon I will have to concentrate on one or the other. ⁹The other night my father made his attitude about what I should do very clear. ¹⁰The most difficult aspect of our cultural differences is the way our family is structured. ¹¹My father is the center of our family, and he expects that I will always listen to him. ¹²Although I am twenty-one years old, I still have a nightly curfew at an hour which I consider insulting. ¹³Also, I am expected to help my mother

continued

> perform certain household chores that I've really come to hate. [14]My father expects me to live at home until I am married to a Vietnamese man. [15]When that happens, he assumes I will obey my husband just as I obey him. [16]I do not want to be a bad daughter, but I want to live like my American female friends.

Fill in the blanks: The first spot where supporting details are needed occurs after sentence number _____. The second spot occurs after sentence number _____. The third spot occurs after sentence number _____.

Base 3: Coherence

Understanding Coherence

Once you have determined that a paragraph is unified and supported, check to see if the writer has a clear and consistent way of organizing the material.

The third base of effective writing is *coherence.* The supporting ideas and sentences in a composition must be organized in a consistent way so that they cohere, or "stick together." Key techniques for tying material together are choosing a clear method of organization (such as time order or emphatic order) and using transitions and other connecting words as signposts.

TIP   To check a paragraph for coherence, ask yourself these questions:

1. Does the paragraph have a clear method of organization?
2. Are transitions and other connecting words used to tie the material together?

Evaluating Paragraphs for Coherence

ACTIVITY 22   **Looking for Organization and Coherence**

Answer the questions about coherence that follow the paragraph below.

Marketing Plan for Campus Child Care Center

[1]In order to effectively market the campus child care center, proper promotion needs to be kept at the top of the priority chart. [2]Most importantly, the expanded Web site should be linked to the campus home page, but should also be available through Bing, Google, and

continued

other common search engines. [3]The Web site should include a welcome message, the mission statement, hours of operation, a link to enrollment information, including forms, and a biography of all the teachers. [4]Word-of-mouth referrals can be increased if a referral bonus is offered. [5]Many families find child care to be very expensive, so offering a bonus that offsets costs would give an incentive for parents to encourage others to use the facility. [6]Open houses are effective; they should be held during peak enrollment times. [7]Holding open houses during times of campus enrollment will increase the likelihood of students learning about the child care center, let students see the facility and meet the staff, and allow students to enroll their children on the spot so the children can start the same day their parents start classes. [8]Using these methods should effectively market the campus child care center.

a. The paragraph should use emphatic order. Write 1 before the idea that seems slightly less important than the other two, 2 before the second most important idea, and 3 before the most important idea.

_____   Expanded Web site

_____   Open houses

_____   Referral bonuses

b. Before which of the three promotional ideas should the transition word *second* be added? _____

c. Before which of the three ideas could the transition *in addition* be added? _____

d. Which words show emphasis in sentence 2? _____

e. What is a synonym for *incentive* in sentence 5? _____

f. What is a synonym for *peak* in sentence 6? _____

Base 4: Sentence Skills

Understanding Sentence Skills

Errors in grammar, punctuation, sentence structure, mechanics, and even formatting can detract greatly from your writing; the fourth base, **sentence skills,** requires that you identify, fix, and avoid these types of mistakes. Error-free sentences allow readers to focus on the content of a paragraph as a whole. Poor grammar and sentence skills can be merely distracting, or they can change the meaning of a sentence entirely; they also lessen a writer's credibility. For instance, a potential employer might think, "If he can't spell the word *political,* does he really have an interest in working on my campaign?"

Part 3 of this book focuses on a wide range of sentence skills. You should review all the skills carefully. Doing so will ensure that you know the most important rules of grammar, punctuation, and usage—rules needed to write clear, error-free sentences.

Checking for Sentence Skills

Sentence skills and the other bases of effective writing are summarized in the following chart and on the inside back cover of the book.

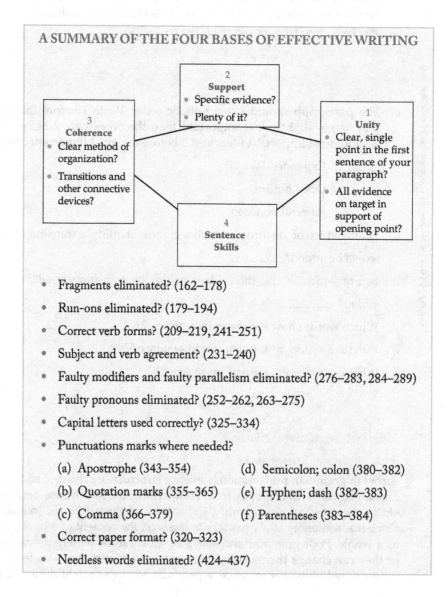

A SUMMARY OF THE FOUR BASES OF EFFECTIVE WRITING

2
Support
- Specific evidence?
- Plenty of it?

3
Coherence
- Clear method of organization?
- Transitions and other connective devices?

1
Unity
- Clear, single point in the first sentence of your paragraph?
- All evidence on target in support of opening point?

4
Sentence Skills

- Fragments eliminated? (162–178)
- Run-ons eliminated? (179–194)
- Correct verb forms? (209–219, 241–251)
- Subject and verb agreement? (231–240)
- Faulty modifiers and faulty parallelism eliminated? (276–283, 284–289)
- Faulty pronouns eliminated? (252–262, 263–275)
- Capital letters used correctly? (325–334)
- Punctuations marks where needed?

    (a) Apostrophe (343–354)   (d) Semicolon; colon (380–382)

    (b) Quotation marks (355–365)   (e) Hyphen; dash (382–383)

    (c) Comma (366–379)   (f) Parentheses (383–384)

- Correct paper format? (320–323)
- Needless words eliminated? (424–437)

Evaluating Paragraphs for Sentence Skills

Identifying Sentence Errors   ACTIVITY 23

Working with a partner, identify the sentence-skills mistakes at the underlined spots in the paragraph that follows. From the box below, choose the letter that describes each mistake and write it in the space provided. The same mistake may appear more than once. Use Part 3: Sentence Skills (pp. 150–435) as a reference.

a. fragment (162–178)	d. apostrophe mistake (343–354)
b. run-on (179–194)	e. faulty parallelism (296–304)
c. mistake in subject-verb agreement (231–240)	

Looking Out for Yourself

It's sad but true: "If you don't look out for yourself, no one else will." For example, some people have a false idea about the power of a college degree, they think that once they possesses the degree, the
$\underset{1}{\qquad}$ $\underset{2}{\qquad}$
world will be waiting on their doorstep. In fact, nobody is likely to be on their doorstep unless, through advance planning, they has prepared
$\underset{3}{\qquad}$
themselves for a career. The kind in which good job opportunities exist.
$\underset{4}{\qquad}$
Even after a person has landed a job, however, a healthy amount of self-interest is needed. People who hide in corners or with hesitation
$\underset{5}{\qquad}$
to let others know about their skills doesn't get promotions or raises. Its
$\underset{6}{\qquad}$ $\underset{7}{\qquad}$
important to take credit for a job well done, whether the job involves writing a report, organized the office filing system, or calming down
$\underset{8}{\qquad}$
an angry customer. Also, people should feel free to ask the boss for a raise. If they work hard and really deserve it. Those who look out
$\underset{9}{\qquad}$
for themselves get the rewards, people who depend on others to help
$\underset{10}{\qquad}$
them along get left behind.

1. _____   2. _____   3. _____   4. _____   5. _____

6. _____   7. _____   8. _____   9. _____   10. _____

ACTIVITY 24   Evaluating Paragraphs for All Four Bases: Unity, Support, Coherence, and Sentence Skills

In this activity, you will evaluate paragraphs in terms of all four bases: unity, support, coherence, and sentence skills. Evaluative comments follow each paragraph below. Circle the letter of the statement that best applies in each case.

1.

Looks Shouldn't Matter, But They Do

Often, job applicants are discriminated against based on physical appearance. First of all, some employers will not hire a man who wears an earring even though a woman who wears earrings is not singled out. In addition, someone with a facial piercing on the lip, nose, or eyebrow is often treated unfairly in the job market. Finally, some employers will not hire a person who has a visible tattoo yet they hire people whose tattoos are hidden.

    a.   The paragraph is not unified.
    b.   The paragraph is not adequately supported.
    c.   The paragraph is not well organized.
    d.   The paragraph does not show a command of sentence skills.
    e.   The paragraph is well written in terms of the four bases.

2.

Getting Better Gas Mileage

There is several ways to get better gas mileage from a car. First of all, a car needs to be properly maintained. Regularly check the air pressure in the tires owing to the fact that underinflated tires can use up more gas. A dirty air filter will also cause a car to consume more fuel. Next, driving efficiently. When on the roadway, people should drive at no more than sixty miles per our. The faster they drive the more gas will be guzzled by the car. At stop signs and traffic lights, avoid sudden starts and stops. Lastly, people need to lighten the car's load. Clean out the trunk and avoid hauling items unnecessarily. Added weight decrease fuel economy. Even though someone cannot control the price at the gas pump; they can control how they use the gas in their fuel tank.

    a.   The paragraph is not unified.
    b.   The paragraph is not adequately supported.
    c.   The paragraph is not well organized.
    d.   The paragraph does not show a command of sentence skills.
    e.   The paragraph is well written in terms of the four bases.

3.

Tips on Bringing Up Children

In some ways, children should be treated as mature people. Adults should not use baby talk with children. Using real words with children helps them develop language skills more quickly. Baby talk makes children feel patronized, frustrated, and confused, for they want to understand and communicate with adults by learning their speech. So animals should be called cows and dogs, not "moo-moos" and "bow-wows." Parents should be consistent when disciplining children. If a parent tells a child, "You cannot have dessert unless you put away your toys," it is important that the parent follow through on the warning. By being consistent, parents will teach children responsibility and give them a stable center around which to grow. Children should be allowed and encouraged to make simple decisions. At a restaurant, children should be allowed to decide what to order. Regarding finances, they should be able to choose if and how they want to spend their money. Parents will thus be helping their children prepare for the complex decisions that they will have to deal with later in life.

a. The paragraph is not unified.
b. The paragraph is not adequately supported.
c. The paragraph is not well organized.
d. The paragraph does not show a command of sentence skills.
e. The paragraph is well written in terms of the four bases.

4.

Recycle and Reuse

People are becoming more aware about the need to reduce, reuse, and recycle, but few are aware of what their garbage can be turned into. Recycling centers are taking more and more items to be sent for recycling and repurposing. For instance, instead of being tossed into landfills, old tires are now being recycled into material for flooring, handbags, jewelry, shoes, and mulch. Plastic bottles are recycled into fleece clothing, carpeting, and "lumber" for decks and bridges. Glass bottles are recycled into new bottles, insulation, and construction materials like tile. However, taking items to the recycling center isn't the only way to turn junk into something new. Old doors can be used as tables, wall decorations, or even headboards for beds. Old CDs and DVDs can be used as wall borders, bird feeders, or even shiny, modern lamps. Out-of-style clothes can be given facelifts with some simple cutting, pinning, and sewing. Plastic bags can be crocheted into water-resistant purses or, with a little creativity, Christmas ornaments! Knowing what ingenious and innovative items garbage can become should encourage anyone to reuse and recycle.

82   PART 2   Writing Effective Paragraphs

a.   The paragraph is not unified.
b.   The paragraph is not adequately supported.
c.   The paragraph is not well organized.
d.   The paragraph does not show a command of sentence skills.
e.   The paragraph is well written in terms of the four bases.

5.

> **Children Are Expensive**
>
> The cost of raising a child keeps increasing. Many families know this fact all too well. For one thing, child care costs are getting higher every year. Parents pay more today for a babysitter or for day care. Teachers' salaries, however, are not going up. For another thing, children's clothing costs more. A pair of children's athletic shoes can easily cost over fifty dollars. Budget-conscious parents should shop at discount and outlet garment stores. In addition, food also costs more. Providing nutritious food is more costly because of rising grocery prices. Sadly, a Happy Meal at McDonald's is often cheaper, but not as nutritious, as a freshly prepared sandwich at home. Health care costs are also getting higher. If a parent is fortunate to have health insurance, that parent may find more of his or her paycheck going toward the monthly premium. Other health-care expenses, such as prescription and over-the-counter drugs, are getting more expensive too.

a.   The paragraph is not unified.
b.   The paragraph is not adequately supported.
c.   The paragraph is not well organized.
d.   The paragraph does not show a command of sentence skills.
e.   The paragraph is well written in terms of the four bases.

WRITING ASSIGNMENT

DESCRIBING SOMETHING VALUABLE

Write a paragraph about a valued material possession. Here are some suggestions:

Car	Appliance
Computer	Cell phone
TV	Photo album
iPod	Piece of clothing
Piece of furniture	Stereo system
Piece of jewelry	Piece of hobby equipment
Camera	Video game console

Your topic sentence should center on the idea that there are several reasons this possession is so important to you. Provide specific examples and details to develop each reason.

Use the following checklist as a guide while you are working on your paragraph:

Yes	No	
_____	_____	Do you begin with a point?
_____	_____	Do you provide relevant, specific details that support the point?
_____	_____	Do you use the words *first of all*, *second*, and *finally* to introduce your three supporting details?
_____	_____	Do you have a closing sentence?
_____	_____	Are your sentences clear and free of obvious errors?

EXPLORING WRITING ONLINE

Visit a favorite Web site of yours and evaluate it for unity, support, coherence, and sentence skills. Then write a paragraph in which you present your evaluation. Use the following questions to help you:

Unity: *Can you easily identify what the Web site's goals are?*

Support: *Does the site contain valuable information, and is that information presented in an effective way?*

Coherence: *Is the site organized and easy to navigate?*

Sentence Skills: *Can you find typos, spelling mistakes, or awkward sentences?*

84   PART 2   Writing Effective Paragraphs

RESPONDING TO IMAGES

Focusing on the third base, *coherence,* describe the organizing principles of this site, as introduced on its home page, shown here.

Nine Patterns of Paragraph Development

CHAPTER PREVIEW

Important Considerations in Paragraph Development

Patterns of Development

Exemplification

Description

Narration

Process

Cause and Effect

Comparison or Contrast

Definition

Division-Classification

Argument

RESPONDING TO IMAGES

These photos capture life right after the 2011 tsunami devastated Japan and one year later. Compare or contrast these photographs, paying attention to which specific details changed or stayed constant after the tsunami struck.

Important Considerations in Paragraph Development

Before you begin work on particular types of paragraphs, there are several general considerations about writing to keep in mind.

Knowing Your Subject

Whenever possible, write on a subject that interests you. You will then find it easier to put more time into your work. Even more important, try to write on a subject that you already know something about. If you do not have direct experience with the subject, you should at least have indirect experience—knowledge gained through thinking, prewriting, reading, or talking about the subject.

If you are asked to write on a topic about which you have no experience or knowledge, you should do whatever research is required to gain the information you need. Without direct or indirect experience, or the information you gain through research, you may not be able to provide the specific evidence needed to develop whatever point you are trying to make. Your writing will be starved for specifics.

Knowing Your Purpose and Audience

The three most common purposes of writing are to inform, to persuade, and to entertain. Each is described briefly below.

- To **inform**—to give information about a subject. Authors who are writing to inform want to provide facts that will explain or teach something to readers. For example, an informative paragraph about sandwiches might begin, "Eating food between two slices of bread—a sandwich—is a practice that has its origins in eighteenth-century England."

- To **persuade**—to convince the reader to agree with the author's point of view on a subject. Authors who are writing to persuade may give facts, but their main goal is to argue or prove a point to readers. A persuasive paragraph about sandwiches might begin, "There are good reasons why every sandwich should be made with whole-grain bread."

- To **entertain**—to amuse and delight; to appeal to the reader's senses and imagination. Authors write to entertain in various ways, through fiction and nonfiction. An entertaining paragraph about sandwiches might begin, "What I wanted was a midnight snack, but what I got was better—the biggest, most magical sandwich in the entire world."

Your audience will be primarily your instructor and sometimes other students. Your instructor is really a symbol of the larger audience you should see yourself writing for—an audience of educated adults who expect you to present your ideas in a clear, direct, organized way. If you can learn to write to persuade or inform such a general audience, you will have accomplished a great deal.

A Note on Tone

It will also be helpful for you to write some paragraphs for a more specific audience. By so doing, you will develop an ability to choose words and adopt a tone of voice that is just right for a given purpose and a given group of people. *Tone* reveals the attitude that a writer has toward a subject. It is expressed through the words and details the writer selects. Just as a speaker's voice can project a range of feelings, a writer's voice can project one or more tones, or feelings: anger, sympathy, hopefulness, sadness, respect, dislike, and so on.

Patterns of Development

Traditionally, writing has been divided into the following patterns of development:

- Exposition
  - *Exemplification*
  - *Process*
  - *Cause and effect*
  - *Comparison or contrast*
  - *Definition*
  - *Division–classification*

- Description

- Narration

- Argumentation

In *exposition*, the writer provides information about and explains a particular subject. Patterns of development within exposition include giving examples (*exemplification*), detailing a *process* of doing or making something, analyzing *causes and effects*, *comparing* or *contrasting*, *defining* a term or concept, and *dividing* something into parts or *classifying* it into categories.

In addition to exposition, three other patterns of development are common: description, narration, and argumentation. A *description* is a verbal picture of a person, place, or thing. In *narration*, a writer tells the story of something that happened. Finally, in *argumentation*, a writer attempts to support a controversial point or defend a position on which there is a difference of opinion.

Each pattern has its own internal logic and provides its own special strategies for imposing order on your ideas.

> **TIP**   As you practice each pattern, you should remember the following:
>
> - Although each paragraph that you write will involve one predominant pattern, very often one or more additional patterns may be involved as well. For instance, the paragraph "My Job at the Crescent Falls Diner and Truck Stop" that you have already read (page 8) presents a series of examples showing why Mike disliked his job. There is also an element of narration, as the writer recounts his experience as a story.
> - Additionally, the paragraph shows how conditions caused this negative effect. No matter which pattern or patterns you use, each paragraph will probably involve some form of argumentation. You will advance a point and then go on to support your point. To convince the reader that your point is valid, you may use a series of examples, or narration, or description, or some other pattern of organization. For instance, a writer could advance the opinion that good horror movies can be easily distinguished from bad horror movies and then supply comparative information about both to support her claim. Much of your writing, in short, will have the purpose of persuading your reader that the idea you have advanced is valid.

Exemplification

In our daily conversations, we often provide *examples*—that is, details, particulars, and specific instances—to explain statements that we make. Consider the several statements and supporting examples in the following box:

Statement	Examples
Wal-Mart was crowded today.	There were at least four carts waiting at each of the checkout counters, and it took me forty-five minutes to get through a line.
The corduroy shirt I bought is poorly made.	When I washed it, the colors began to fade, one button cracked and another fell off, a shoulder seam opened, and the sleeves shrank almost two inches.
My son Peter is unreliable.	If I depend on him to turn off a pot of beans in ten minutes, the family is likely to eat burned beans. If I ask him to turn down the thermostat before he goes to bed, the heat is likely to stay on all night.

In each case, the examples help us *see for ourselves* the truth of the statement that has been made. In paragraphs, too, explanatory examples help the audience fully understand a point. Lively, specific examples also add interest to a piece of writing.

A Paragraph to Consider

Proposal for New FEMA Building

[1]The college engineering department has designed a FEMA building that will be used to enhance the college community in four distinct ways. [2]Currently, the theater department has no place to perform, so this facility will be designed to include a black box theater. [3]When the room is set up as a theater, it will be able to hold 250 people. [4]All seating and staging in the theater will be electronically and mechanically controlled, so the room can be quickly cleared in case of emergency. [5]Also, the facility will serve the art and dance programs because a dance studio and art gallery will be built on either side of the black box. [6]Moreover, all three facilities could serve as additional meeting venues. [7]A perk for the surrounding community is that they will be able to rent the space. [8]Most importantly, the building will serve as a FEMA-approved safe building that can hold 1500 people. [9]The concrete walls will be 24 inches thick, and the ceiling will be reinforced to withstand an EF5 tornado. [10]There will be several entrances to the black box portion of the building, and in times of adverse weather, the entrances can be remotely unlocked to allow for quick entry. [11]Adding the FEMA building to the campus will not only offer a safe spot during adverse weather, but it will enhance the college's arts and theater programs and provide additional meeting venues.

About Unity

QUESTIONS

1. Which sentence in "Proposal for New FEMA Building" is irrelevant to the point that the new building will directly enhance the college? *(Write the sentence number here.)*

   _____

About Support

2. How many specific examples are given that show that the new FEMA building will directly enhance the college?

   _____ two _____ three _____ four _____ five _____ six

About Coherence

3. What are six transition words and phrases used in "Proposal for New FEMA Building"?

   _____ _____ _____ _____ _____ _____

90   PART 2   Writing Effective Paragraphs

Writing an Exemplification Paragraph

PORTRAYING A SELFISH PERSON

Complete this unfinished paragraph (in the following box), which has as its topic sentence, "My husband Roger is a selfish person." Provide the supporting details needed to develop the examples of Roger's selfishness. The first example has been done for you.

A Selfish Person

My husband Roger is a selfish person. For one thing, he refuses to move out of the city, even though it is a bad place to raise the children. *We inherited some money when my parents died, and it might be enough for a down payment on a small house in a nearby town. But Roger says he would miss his buddies in the neighborhood.*

_____

Also, when we go on vacation, we always go where Roger wants to go. _____

_____

_____

Another example of Roger's selfishness is that he always spends any budget money that is left over. _____

_____

_____

_____

Finally, Roger leaves all the work of caring for the children to me.

_____

_____

_____

_____

PREWRITING

a. On a separate piece of paper, jot down a couple of answers for each of the following questions:

   • What specific vacations did the family go on because Roger wanted to go? Write down particular places, length of stay, time of year.

What vacations has the family never gone on (for example, to visit the wife's relatives), even though the wife wanted to?

- What specific items has Roger bought for himself (rather than for the whole family's use) with leftover budget money?

- What chores and duties involved in the everyday caring for the children has Roger never done?

Your instructor may ask you to work with one or two other students in generating the details needed to develop the three examples in the paragraph. The groups may then be asked to read their details aloud, with the class deciding which details are the most effective for each example.

Here, and in general in your writing, try to generate *more* supporting material than you need. You are then in a position to choose the most convincing details for your paper.

b. Read over the details you have generated and decide which sound most effective. Jot down additional details as they occur to you.

c. Take your best details, reshape them as needed, and use them to complete the paragraph about Roger.

REVISING: PEER REVIEW

Read the paragraph to a classmate or friend with these questions in mind to make sure you have covered the four bases of effective writing:

CHECKLIST FOR EXEMPLIFICATION: THE FOUR BASES

ABOUT *UNITY*

✔ Do all of the examples I provide support the central idea that Roger is selfish?

ABOUT *SUPPORT*

✔ Are there enough examples to make my point about Roger and convince others to agree with me?

✔ Do I appeal to my readers' senses with vivid, specific examples?

ABOUT *COHERENCE*

✔ Have I presented the examples in my paragraph in the most effective order?

ABOUT *SENTENCE SKILLS*

✔ Have I used specific rather than general words?

✔ Are my sentences varied in length and structure?

✔ Have I checked for spelling and other sentence skills, as listed on the inside back cover of the book?

Continue revising your work until you and your reader can answer *yes* to all these questions.

92   PART 2   Writing Effective Paragraphs

Imagine that you are a restaurant manager who needs to write a paragraph-long article for the training manual about high-quality customer service. Explain this concept by providing specific examples so that your employees understand how important customer service is in the competitive food service industry.

Description

When you describe something or someone, you give your readers a picture in words. To make this "word picture" as vivid and real as possible, you must observe and record specific details that appeal to your readers' senses (sight, hearing, taste, smell, and touch). More than any other type of writing, a descriptive paragraph needs sharp, colorful details.

Here is a description in which only the sense of sight is used:

> A rug covers the living-room floor.

In contrast, here is a description rich in sense impressions:

> A thick, reddish-brown shag rug is laid wall to wall across the living-room floor. The long, curled fibers of the shag seem to whisper as you walk through them in your bare feet, and when you squeeze your toes into the deep covering, the soft fibers push back at you with a spongy resilience.

Sense impressions include sight (*thick, reddish-brown shag rug; laid wall to wall; walk through them in your bare feet; squeeze your toes into the deep covering; push back*), hearing (*whisper*), and touch (*bare feet, soft fibers, spongy resilience*). The sharp, vivid images provided by the sensory details give us a clear picture of the rug and enable us to share the writer's experience.

A Paragraph to Consider

My Teenage Son's Room

¹I push open the door with difficulty. ²The doorknob is loose and has to be jiggled just right before the catch releases from the doorjamb. ³Furthermore, as I push at the door, it runs into a basketball shoe lying on the floor. ⁴I manage to squeeze in through the narrow opening. ⁵I am immediately aware of a pungent odor in the room, most of which is coming from the closet, to my right. ⁶That's the location of a white wicker clothes hamper, heaped with grass-stained jeans, sweat-stained T-shirts, and smelly socks. ⁷But the half-eaten burrito, lying dried and unappetizing on the bedside table across the room, contributes a bit of aroma, as does the glass of curdled, sour milk sitting on the sunny

continued

CHAPTER 4   Nine Patterns of Paragraph Development   93

windowsill. [8]To my left, the small wire cage on Greg's desk is also fragrant, but pleasantly. [9]From its nest of sweet-smelling cedar chips, the gerbil peers out at me with its bright eyes, its tiny claws scratching against the cage wall. [10]The floor around the wastebasket that is next to the desk is surrounded by what appears to be a sprinkling of snowballs. [11]They're actually old wadded-up school papers, and I can picture Greg sitting on his bed, crushing them into balls and aiming them at the "basket"—the trash can. [12]I glance at the bed across from the desk and chuckle because pillows stuffed under the tangled nest of blankets make it look as if someone is still sleeping there, though I know Greg is in history class right now. [13]I step carefully through the room, trying to walk through the obstacle course of science-fiction paperbacks, a wristwatch, sports magazines, and a dust-covered computer on which my son stacks empty soda cans. [14]I leave everything as I find it, but tape a note to Greg's door saying, "Isn't it about time to clean up?"

About Unity

1. Does this paragraph have a topic sentence?

   _____

About Support

2. Label as *sight, touch, hearing,* or *smell* all the sensory details in the following sentences.

   That's the location of a white wicker clothes hamper, heaped with

   grass-stained jeans, sweat-stained T-shirts, and smelly socks.

About Coherence

3. Spatial signals (*above, next to, to the right,* and so on) are often used to help organize details in a descriptive paragraph. List four space signals that appear in "My Teenage Son's Room":

   _____

QUESTIONS

Writing a Descriptive Paragraph

DESCRIBING A PARTICULAR ROOM

Write a paragraph describing a certain person's room. Use as your topic sentence "I could tell by looking at the room that a _____ lived there." There are many kinds of people who could be the focus for such

WRITING ASSIGNMENT

a paragraph. You can select any one of the following, or think of another type of person.

Photographer	Music lover	Carpenter
Cook	TV addict	Baby
Student	Camper	Cat or dog lover
Musician	Hacker	World traveler
Hunter	Cheerleader	Drug addict
Slob	Football player	Little boy or girl
Outdoors person	Actor	Alcoholic
Doctor	Dancer	Swimmer

PREWRITING

a. After choosing a topic, spend a few minutes making sure it will work. Prepare a list of all the details you can think of that support the topic. For example, a student who planned to describe a soccer player's room made this list:

soccer balls

shin guards

posters of professional soccer teams

soccer trophies

shirt printed with team name and number

autographed soccer ball

medals and ribbons

photos of player's own team

sports clippings

radio that looks like soccer ball

soccer socks

soccer shorts

If you don't have enough details, choose another type of person. Check your new choice by listing details before committing yourself to the topic.

b. You may want to use other prewriting techniques, such as freewriting or questioning, to develop more details for your topic. As you continue prewriting, keep the following in mind:

- Everything in the paragraph should support your point. For example, if you are writing about a soccer player's room, every detail should serve to show that the person who lives in that room plays and loves soccer. Other details—for example, the person's computer, tropical fish tank, or daily "to-do" list—should be omitted.

- Description depends on the use of specific rather than general descriptive words. For example:

General	Specific
Mess on the floor	The obstacle course of science-fiction paperbacks, a wristwatch, sports magazines, and a dust-covered computer on which my son stacks empty soda cans
Ugly turtle tub	Large plastic tub of dirty, stagnant-looking water containing a few motionless turtles
Bad smell	Unpleasant mixture of strong chemical deodorizers, urine-soaked newspapers, and musty sawdust
Nice skin	Soft, velvety brown skin

Remember that you want your readers to experience the room vividly. Your words should be as detailed as a clear photograph, giving readers a real feel for the room. Appeal to as many senses as possible. Most of your description will involve the sense of sight, but you may be able to include details about touch, hearing, and smell as well.

- Spatial order is a good way to organize a descriptive paragraph. Move as a visitor's eye might move around the room, from right to left or from larger items to smaller ones. Here are a few transition words of the sort that show spatial relationships.

to the left	across from	on the opposite side
to the right	above	nearby
next to	below	

Such transitions will help prevent you—and your reader—from getting lost as the description proceeds.

c. Before you write, see if you can make a scratch outline based on your list. Here is one possible outline of the paragraph about the soccer player's room. Note that the details are organized according to spatial order—from the edges of the room in toward the center.

Topic sentence: I could tell by looking at the room that a soccer player lived there.

1. Walls
2. Bookcase
3. Desk
4. Chair
5. Floor

d. Then proceed to write a first draft of your paragraph.

96   PART 2   Writing Effective Paragraphs

REVISING: PEER REVIEW

Read your descriptive paragraph slowly out loud to a friend or classmate. Ask the friend to close his or her eyes and try to picture the room as you read. Read it out loud a second time. To ensure you have covered the four bases of effective writing, ask your friend to answer these questions:

CHECKLIST FOR DESCRIPTION: THE FOUR BASES

ABOUT *UNITY*

✔ Does every detail in the paragraph support the topic sentence? Here's one way to find out: Ask your friend to imagine omitting the key word or words (in the case of our example, *soccer player*) in your topic sentence. Would readers know what word should fit in that empty space?

ABOUT *SUPPORT*

✔ Are the details specific and vivid rather than general?

✔ Has the writer included details that appeal to as many senses as possible?

ABOUT *COHERENCE*

✔ Does the paragraph follow a logical spatial order?

✔ Has the writer used transitions (such as *on top of, beside,* and *to the left of*) to help the reader follow that order?

ABOUT *SENTENCE SKILLS*

✔ Has the writer carefully proofread his or her paragraph, using the list on the inside back cover of the book, and corrected all sentence-skills mistakes, including spelling?

Continue revising your work until you and your reader can answer *yes* to all these questions.

BEYOND THE CLASSROOM (Work)

Description

Imagine that you are an interior designer. Write a paragraph describing a design for one of the following: a child's bedroom, a kitchen, a small restaurant, a porch, or a bakery. In your prewriting, you might list all the relevant needs of the people who live or work in the space you are designing. Consider issues such as storage space, appropriate lighting and colors, and the first thing people should or would notice when they walk in. Then put all the parts together so that they work well as a whole. Use a spatial order in your paragraph to help readers "see" your room.

Narration

At times we make a statement clear by relating in detail something that has happened. In the story we tell, we present the details in the order in which they happened. A person might say, for example, "I was embarrassed yesterday," and then go on to illustrate the statement with the following narrative:

> I was hurrying across campus to get to a class. It had rained heavily all morning, so I was hopscotching my way around puddles in the pathway. I called to two friends ahead to wait for me, and right before I caught up to them, I came to a large puddle that covered the entire path. I had to make a quick choice of either stepping into the puddle or trying to jump over it. I jumped, wanting to seem cool, since my friends were watching, but didn't clear the puddle. Water splashed everywhere, drenching my shoe, sock, and pants cuff, and spraying the pants of my friends as well. "Well done, Dave!" they said. My embarrassment was all the greater because I had tried to look so casual.

The speaker's details have made his moment of embarrassment vivid and real for us, and we can see and understand just why he felt as he did.

A Paragraph to Consider

Francesca's Goal Setting Worked for Her!

[1]Getting a college degree is a goal for many people, but setting smaller goals leading to the larger goal is an important way to maintain motivation. [2]One student, Francesca, did a great job keeping herself motivated by setting small study goals. [3]At the start of each semester, she met with her advisor to set up her schedule and then she carefully planned her study time. [4]Because she wanted grades of B or higher, Francesca mapped out a way to study at least three hours a week for each class she was taking. [5]Once she planned her study time, she made sure that the time was productive. [6]She loved to study in her office because it was bright hot pink. [7]Despite the temptation to just skim over her homework or put off an assignment because she knew the instructor wasn't going to collect it, Francesca forced herself to focus and work harder than she thought she should. [8]When she managed to study successfully and keep her grades high, she rewarded herself with things like seeing a movie, getting together with a friend, or sleeping in on the weekend. [9]Whenever she didn't meet her study goals, Francesca reflected on what went wrong that week and worked to avoid repeating that behavior. [10]There were some weeks when circumstances beyond her control hindered her progress, so she used the experiences as learning opportunities, met with her instructors to get back on track, and refocused herself the following week. [11]By setting these small study goals each week and each semester, Francesca successfully finished college and earned a degree.

QUESTIONS

About Unity

1. Which sentence in this paragraph should be omitted in the interest of unity? *(Write the sentence number here.)*

_____

About Support

2. What do you think is the best (or most real and vivid) detail or image in the paragraph "Francesca's Goal Setting Worked for Her!"?

_____

_____

About Coherence

3. Does the paragraph use time order or emphatic order to organize details?

_____

4. What are at least three transition words used in this paragraph?

_____ _____ _____ _____

Writing a Narrative Paragraph

RATIONALIZING AN EMOTION

WRITING ASSIGNMENT

Write a paragraph about an experience in which a certain emotion was predominant. The emotion might be fear, pride, satisfaction, embarrassment, or any of these:

Frustration	Sympathy	Shyness
Love	Bitterness	Disappointment
Sadness	Violence	Happiness
Terror	Surprise	Jealousy
Shock	Nostalgia	Anger
Relief	Loss	Hate
Envy	Silliness	Nervousness

The experience you write about should be limited in time. Another good way to write an effective narrative paragraph and to bring an event to life for your readers is to include some dialogue. Words that you said, or that someone else said, help make a situation come alive. First, though, be sure to check the section on quotation marks on pages 355–365.

PREWRITING

a. Begin by freewriting. Think of an experience or event that caused you to feel a certain emotion strongly. Then spend ten minutes writing freely about the experience. Do not worry at this point about spelling or

CHAPTER 4   Nine Patterns of Paragraph Development   99

grammar or putting things in the right order. Instead, just try to get down all the details you can think of that seem related to the experience.

b. This preliminary writing will help you decide whether your topic is promising enough to develop further. If it is not, choose another emotion and repeat step *a*. If it does seem promising, do two things:

   • First, write your topic sentence, underlining the emotion you will focus on. For example, "My first day in kindergarten was one of the *scariest* days of my life."

   • Second, make up a list of all the details involved in the experience. Then number these details according to the order in which they occurred.

c. Referring to your list of details, write a rough draft of your paragraph. Use time signals such as *first, then, after, next, while, during,* and *finally* to help connect details as you move from the beginning to the middle to the end of your narrative. Be sure to include not only what happened but also how you felt about what was going on.

REVISING: PEER REVIEW

Put your first draft away for a day or so. When you return to your paragraph, share it with a friend or classmate whose judgment you trust. Go over the following questions with your reader to make sure you have covered the four bases of effective writing:

CHECKLIST FOR NARRATION: THE FOUR BASES

ABOUT *UNITY*

✔ Does my topic sentence clearly state what emotion the experience made me feel?

✔ Are there any off-topic sentences I should eliminate for the sake of paragraph unity?

ABOUT *SUPPORT*

✔ Have I included some dialogue to make the experience come alive?

✔ Have I explained how I felt as the experience occurred?

ABOUT *COHERENCE*

✔ Have I used time order to narrate the experience from beginning to end?

✔ Have I used time signals to connect one detail to the next?

ABOUT *SENTENCE SKILLS*

✔ Have I carefully proofread my paragraph, using the list on the inside back cover of the book, and corrected all sentence-skills mistakes, including spelling?

✔ Is the first-person point of view (I) in my paragraph consistent?

✔ Did I use verb tenses consistently and correctly? (This is especially important when relaying a story.)

Continue revising your work until you and your reader can answer *yes* to all these questions.

BEYOND THE CLASSROOM Personal

Narration

Imagine that one of your oldest friends has to make a difficult decision of some kind. Narrate a relevant story from your own experience (or the experience of someone you know) that will help your friend carefully weigh the decision he or she must make. In your paragraph, include a comment or two about how your story relates to your friend's situation. Throughout, try to be helpful without being condescending. You can also be entertaining, as long as you are careful to stay sensitive to the problem at hand.

Process

Every day we perform many activities that are *processes*—that is, series of steps carried out in a definite order. Many of these processes are familiar and automatic: for example, tying shoelaces, changing bed linen, using a vending machine, and starting a car. We are thus seldom aware of the sequence of steps making up each activity. In other cases, such as when we are asked for directions to a particular place, or when we try to read and follow the directions for a new table game, we may be painfully conscious of the whole series of steps involved in the process.

TIP In process writing, you are often giving instruction to the reader, so the pronoun *you* can appropriately be used. As a general rule, though, do not use *you* in your writing.

A Paragraph to Consider

How to Harass an Instructor

¹Here are the steps my friend Kyle takes to harass his instructors. ²First of all, he shows up late so that he can interrupt the beginning of the instructor's presentation. ³In a normal tone of voice, as he sits down, he starts greeting his friends and scraping his chair as loudly as possible while making himself comfortable. ⁴Then he just sits there and does anything but pay attention. ⁵When the instructor sees that he is not involved in the class, she may pop a quick question, probably hoping to embarrass him. ⁶In a loud voice, Kyle then replies, "I DON'T KNOW THE ANSWER." ⁷This declaration of ignorance typically throws the instructor off guard. ⁸She may

continued

CHAPTER 4   Nine Patterns of Paragraph Development   101

then ask Kyle why he doesn't know the answer, and he says, "I don't even know what page we're on" or "I thought the assignment was boring, so I didn't do it." [9]After the instructor calls on someone else, Kyle gets up loudly from his seat, walks to the front of the classroom, and demands to be excused for an emergency visit to the washroom. [10]He stays there at least fifteen minutes and takes his time coming back. [11]On the way back, he finds a vending machine and buys himself his favorite chips snack because he deserves it. [12]When the instructor asks him where he's been, he simply ignores the question and goes to his seat. [13]He then flops into his chair, slouching back and extending his legs as far out as possible. [14]When the instructor informs him of the assignment that the class is working on, he heaves an exaggerated sigh and very slowly opens up his book and starts turning the pages. [15]About a half hour before class is over, he begins to look at the clock every few minutes. [16]Ten minutes before dismissal time, he starts noisily packing up his books and papers. [17]Then he gets up and walks to the door a couple of minutes before the class is supposed to end. [18]At this point, the instructor may look at him in wonder and loudly declare to the class that she might have been better off going into business instead of education.

About Unity

1. Which sentence should be eliminated in the interest of paragraph unity? (*Write the sentence number here.*)

   _____

About Support

2. After which sentence in "How to Harass an Instructor" are supporting details (examples) needed?

   _____

About Coherence

3. Does this paragraph use time order or emphatic order?

   _____

QUESTIONS

Writing a Process Paragraph

EXPLAINING A PROCESS

Choose one of the following topics to write about in a process paragraph.

　　How to feed a family on a budget

　　How to break up with a boyfriend or girlfriend

How to balance a checkbook

How to change a car or bike tire

How to get rid of house or garden pests, such as mice, roaches, or wasps

How to play a simple game, such as checkers

How to parallel park

How to shorten a skirt or pants

How to meet new people, for either dating or friendship

How to plant a garden

How to get started on Facebook

How to fix a leaky faucet, a clogged drain, or the like

How to build a campfire or start a fire in a fireplace

How to study for an important exam

How to conduct a yard or garage sale

How to wash dishes efficiently, clean a bathroom, or do laundry

How to create the perfect online dating profile

PREWRITING

a. Begin by freewriting on your topic for ten minutes. Do not worry about spelling, grammar, organization, or other matters of form. Just write whatever comes into your head regarding the topic. Keep writing for more than ten minutes if ideas keep coming to you. This freewriting will give you a base of raw material to draw from during the next phase of your work on the paragraph. After freewriting, you should have a sense of whether there is enough material available for you to write a process paragraph about the topic. If so, continue as explained below. If there is not enough material, choose another topic and freewrite about *it* for ten minutes.

b. Write a clear, direct topic sentence stating the process you are going to describe. For instance, if you are going to describe a way to study for major exams, your topic sentence might be "My study-skills in-structor has suggested a good way to study for major exams." Or you can state in your topic sentence the process and the number of steps involved: "My technique for building a campfire involves four main steps."

c. List all the steps you can think of that may be included in the process. At this point, don't worry about how each step fits or whether two steps overlap. Here, for example, is the list prepared by a student who is writing about how to sneak into the house at night.

Quiet on stairs

Come in after Dad's asleep

House is freezing at night

Bring key

Know which steps to avoid

Lift up front door

Late parties on Saturday night

Don't turn on bathroom light

Avoid squeaky spots on floor

Get into bed quietly

Undress quietly

d. Number your items in the order in which they occur; strike out items that do not fit in the list; add others that come to mind. The student writer did this step as follows:

~~Quiet on stairs~~

2 Come in after Dad's asleep

~~House is freezing at night~~

1 Bring key

5 Know which steps to avoid

3 Lift up front door

~~Late parties on Saturday night~~

6 Don't turn on bathroom light

4 Avoid squeaky spots on floor

8 Get into bed quietly

7 Undress quietly

e. Use your list as a guide to write the first draft of your paragraph. As you write, try to think of additional details that will support your opening sentence. Do not expect to finish your paragraph in one draft. After you complete your first rough draft, in fact, you should be ready to write a series of drafts as you work toward the goals of unity, support, and coherence.

REVISING: PEER REVIEW

After you have written the first draft of your paragraph, set it aside for a while if you can. Then read it out loud, either to yourself or (better yet) to a friend or classmate who will be honest with you about how it sounds.

Reexamine your paragraph with these questions in mind to make sure you have covered the four bases of effective writing:

CHECKLIST FOR PROCESS: THE FOUR BASES

ABOUT *UNITY*

✔ An effective process composition describes a series of events in a way that is clear and easy to follow. Are the steps in your paragraph described in a clear, logical way?

ABOUT *SUPPORT*

✔ Does your paragraph explain every necessary step so that a reader could perform the task described?

ABOUT *COHERENCE*

✔ Have you used transitions such as *first, next, also, then, after, now, during,* and *finally* to make the paper move smoothly from one step to another?

ABOUT *SENTENCE SKILLS*

✔ Is the point of view consistent? For example, if you begin by writing "This is how I got rid of mice" (first person), do not switch to "You must buy the right traps" (second person). Write your paragraph consistently from first-, second-, or third-person point of view—do not jump back and forth among them.

✔ Have you corrected any sentence-skills mistakes that you noticed while reading the paragraph out loud? Have you checked the composition for sentence skills, including spelling, as listed on the inside back cover of this book?

Continue revising your work until you and your reader can answer *yes* to all these questions.

BEYOND THE CLASSROOM   (Work)

Process

Imagine that you have to train someone to take your place in any job you've held (or currently hold); if you have never held a job, you can train this person to take your place as a student. Write a process paragraph that describes what a day on the job entails. Break the day's activities down into steps, making sure to include what advance preparation your replacement might need.

Cause and Effect

What caused Pat to drop out of school? Why are soap operas so popular? Why does our football team do so poorly each year? How has retirement affected Dad? What effects does divorce have on children? Every day we ask such questions and look for answers. We realize that situations have causes and effects—good or bad. By examining causes and effects, we seek to understand and explain things.

A Paragraph to Consider

New Puppy in the House

¹Buying a new puppy can have significant effects on a household. ²For one thing, the puppy keeps the entire family awake for at least two solid weeks. ³Every night when the puppy is placed in its box, it begins to howl, yip, and whine. ⁴Even after the lights go out and the house quiets down, the puppy continues to moan. ⁵A second effect is that the puppy tortures the family by destroying material possessions. ⁶Every day something different is damaged. ⁷Family members find chewed belts and shoes, gnawed table legs, and ripped sofa cushions leaking stuffing. ⁸In addition, the puppy often misses the paper during the paper-training stage of life, thus making the house smell like the public restroom at a city bus station. ⁹Maybe the most serious problem, though, is that the puppy causes family arguments. ¹⁰Parents argue with children about who is supposed to feed and walk the dog. ¹¹Children argue about who gets to play with the puppy first. ¹²Puppies are adorable, and no child can resist their charm. ¹³Everyone argues about who left socks and shoes around for the puppy to find. ¹⁴These continual arguments, along with the effects of sleeplessness and the loss of valued possessions, can really disrupt a household. ¹⁵Only when the puppy gets a bit older does the household settle back to normal.

About Unity

1. Which sentence does not support the opening idea and should be omitted? (*Write the sentence number here.*)

   _____

About Support

2. How many effects of bringing a new puppy into the house are given in this paragraph?

   _____ one _____ two _____ three _____four

About Coherence

3. What words signal the effect that the author feels may be the most important?

   _____

QUESTIONS

Writing a Cause-and-Effect Paragraph

WRITING ASSIGNMENT

(Academic)

DEVELOPING AN OUTLINE

Choose one of the following three topic sentences and brief outlines. Each is made up of three supporting points (causes or effects). Your task is to turn the topic sentence and outline into a cause-and-effect paragraph.

OPTION 1
Topic sentence: There are several reasons why parenthood makes people more responsible.
(1) Ensure that children's needs are met (*cause*)
(2) Cannot think only of themselves (*cause*)
(3) Provide children with a better life (*cause*)

OPTION 2
Topic sentence: My divorce has changed my life in positive ways.
(1) Enrolled in college (*effect*)
(2) More quality time with children (*effect*)
(3) Began exercising regularly (*effect*)

OPTION 3
Topic sentence: Lack of sleep makes daily life more difficult.
(1) Difficulty focusing on homework (*cause*)
(2) Irritable all the time (*cause*)
(3) More prone to colds and the flu (*cause*)

PREWRITING

a. After you've chosen the option that appeals to you most, jot down all the details you can think of that might go under each of the supporting points. Use separate paper for your lists. Don't worry yet about whether you can use all the items—your goal is to generate more material than you need. Here, for example, are some of the details generated by the author of "New Puppy in the House" to back up her supporting points.

Topic sentence: Having a new puppy disrupts a household.

1. Keeps family awake
   a. Whines at night
   b. Howls
   c. Loss of sleep
2. Destroys possessions
   a. Chews belts and shoes
   b. Chews furniture
   c. Tears up toys it's supposed to fetch
3. Has accidents in house
   a. Misses paper
   b. Disgusting cleanup
   c. Makes house smell bad

4. Causes arguments
    a. Arguments about walking dog
    b. Arguments about feeding dog
    c. Arguments about who gets to play with dog
    d. Arguments about vet bills

b. Now go through the details you have generated and decide which are most effective. Strike out the ones you decide are not worth using. Do other details occur to you? If so, jot them down as well.

c. Now you are ready to write your paragraph. Begin the paragraph with the topic sentence you chose. Make sure to develop each of the supporting points from the outline into a complete sentence, and then back it up with the best of the details you have generated.

REVISING: PEER REVIEW

Review your paragraph with a friend or classmate. The two of you should keep these questions in mind to make sure you have covered the four bases of effective writing:

CHECKLIST FOR CAUSE AND EFFECT: THE FOUR BASES

ABOUT *UNITY*

✔ Have you begun the paragraph with the topic sentence provided?

✔ Are any sentences in your paragraph not directly relevant to this topic sentence?

ABOUT *SUPPORT*

✔ Is each supporting point stated in a complete sentence?

✔ Have you provided effective details to back up each supporting point?

ABOUT *COHERENCE*

✔ Have you used transitions such as *in addition, another thing,* and *also* to make the relationships between the sentences clear?

ABOUT *SENTENCE SKILLS*

✔ Have you avoided wordiness?

✔ Have you proofread the paragraph for sentence-skills errors, including spelling, as listed on the inside back cover of the book?

Continue revising your work until you and your reader can answer *yes* to all these questions.

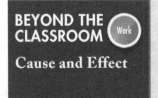

BEYOND THE CLASSROOM Work

Cause and Effect

Imagine that you are a retail store manager and must write a letter to one of your employees. Not only is this person a poor salesperson but also he or she has a negative attitude and lacks leadership qualities. Write a paragraph that explains three ways in which this person has negatively impacted the company, and then write another paragraph in which you ask this person to help you understand the causes of his or her behavior and attitude.

Comparison or Contrast

Comparison and contrast are two everyday thought processes. When we *compare* two things, we show how they are similar; when we *contrast* two things, we show how they are different. We might compare or contrast two brand-name products (for example, Nike versus Adidas running shoes), two television shows, two instructors, two jobs, two friends, or two courses of action we could take in a given situation. The purpose of comparing and contrasting is to understand each of the two things more clearly and, at times, to make judgments about them.

There are two common methods, or formats, of development in a comparison or contrast paper. One format presents the details *one side at a time*. The other presents the details *point by point*.

Two Paragraphs to Consider

Read these sample paragraphs of comparison or contrast and then answer the questions that follow.

Academic

Two Writers: Dickens and King

[1]Few people would compare Charles Dickens with Stephen King, but the authors have a lot more in common than might first appear. [2]Neither author started out as a novel writer. [3]Dickens first started working as a freelance court reporter at Doctors' Commons, a civil court in London. [4]King worked as a reporter for the University of Maine at Orono's school newspaper. [5]Both Dickens and King published short stories first. [6]Dickens started selling short stories in 1836, and in 1837 he published *The Pickwick Papers*. [7]The success of this book led Dickens to a full-time job writing. [8]King first started selling short stories in 1967, and in 1974 when his first novel, *Carrie*, was published, King became a full-time writer. [9]Both authors are considered writers of their time. [10]Dickens's stories were very popular with upper-, middle-, and lower-class citizens. [11]His books spanned the class system because he focused on humanity, facing adversity, dealing with dishonest people, and overcoming social injustice. [12]Like Dickens, King's novels are also popular with a variety of people: teenagers, adults, men, and women. [13]His stories reflect modern times, often with a scary tone, all the while allowing the reader to observe humanity, controversy, and social injustice. [14]Charles Dickens and Stephen King may have lived more than a hundred years apart, but their similarities span the decades.

Mike and Helen

[1]Mike and Helen, a married couple we know, look very much alike. They are both short, dark-haired, and slightly pudgy. [2]Like his wife, Mike has a good sense of humor. [3]Both Mike and Helen can be charming when they want to be, and they seem to handle small crises in a calm, cool way. [4]A problem such as an overflowing washer, a stalled car, or a sick child is not a cause for panic; they take such events in stride. [5]In contrast to Helen, though, Mike tends to be disorganized. [6]He is late for appointments and unable to keep important documents where he can find them. [7]Also unlike Helen, Mike often holds a grudge. [8]Another difference between these two is how they like to spend their free time; while Mike enjoys swimming, camping, and fishing, Helen prefers to stay inside and read or play chess.

About Unity

1. Which paragraph lacks a topic sentence?

   _____

About Support

2. Which paragraph provides more complete support?

   _____

About Coherence

3. What method of development (one side at a time or point by point) is used in "Mike and Helen"?

   _____

4. What method of development is used in "Two Writers: Dickens and King"?

   _____

QUESTIONS

RESPONDING TO IMAGES

Compare or contrast these two photographs of men cooking.

Writing a Comparison or Contrast Paragraph

FOCUSING ON TWO

WRITING ASSIGNMENT

Write a comparison or contrast paragraph on one of the following topics:

Two holidays	Two characters in the same movie or TV show
Two instructors	
Two children	Two homes
Two kinds of eaters	Two neighborhoods
Two drivers	Two cartoon strips
Two coworkers	Two cars
Two members of a team (or two teams)	Two friends
Two singers or groups	Two crises
Two pets	Two bosses or supervisors
Two parties	Two magazines
Two jobs	

PREWRITING

a. Choose your topic, the two subjects you will write about.

b. Decide whether your paragraph will *compare* the two subjects (discuss their similarities), *contrast* them (discuss their differences), or do both. If you choose to write about differences, you might write about how a musical group you enjoy differs from a musical group you dislike. You might discuss important differences between two employers you have had or between two neighborhoods you've lived in. You might contrast a job you've had in a car factory with a job you've had as a receptionist.

c. Write a direct topic sentence for your paragraph. Here's an example: "my job in a car-parts factory was very different from my job as a receptionist."

d. Come up with at least three strong points to support your topic sentence. If you are contrasting two jobs, for example, your points might be that they differed greatly (1) in their physical setting, (2) in the skills they required, and (3) in the people they brought you into contact with.

e. Use your topic sentence and supporting points to create a scratch outline for your paragraph. For the paragraph about jobs, the outline would look like this:

Topic sentence: My job in a car-parts factory was very different from my job as a receptionist.

1. The jobs differed in physical setting.
2. The jobs differed in the skills they required.
3. The jobs differed in the people they brought me into contact with.

f.   Under each of your supporting points, jot down as many details as occur to you. Don't worry yet about whether the details all fit perfectly or whether you will be able to use them all. Your goal is to generate a wealth of material to draw on. An example:

Topic sentence: My job in a car-parts factory was very different from my job as a receptionist.

1.   The jobs differed in physical setting.

Factory loud and dirty

Office clean and quiet

Factory full of machines, hunks of metal, tools

Office full of desks, files, computers

Factory smelled of motor oil

Office smelled of new carpet

Windows in factory too high and grimy to look out of

Office had clean windows onto street

2.   The jobs differed in the skills and behavior they required.

Factory required physical strength

Office required mental activity

Didn't need to be polite in factory

Had to be polite in office

Didn't need to think much for self in factory

Constantly had to make decisions in office

3.   The jobs differed in the people they brought me into contact with.

In factory, worked with same crew every day

In office, saw constant stream of new customers

Most coworkers in factory had high school education or less

Many coworkers and clients in office well educated

Coworkers in factory spoke variety of languages

Rarely heard anything but English in office

g.   Decide which format you will use to develop your paragraph: one side at a time or point by point. Either is acceptable; it is up to you to decide which you prefer. The important thing is to be consistent: Whichever format you choose, be sure to use it throughout the entire paragraph.

h.   Write the first draft of your paragraph.

REVISING: PEER REVIEW

Put your composition away for a day or so. You will return to it with a fresh perspective and a better ability to critique what you have written. Share your paragraph with a friend or fellow classmate. Together, read your

112 PART 2 Writing Effective Paragraphs

paragraph with these questions in mind to make sure you have covered the four bases of effective writing:

CHECKLIST FOR COMPARISON OR CONTRAST: THE FOUR BASES

ABOUT *UNITY*

✔ Does your topic sentence make it clear what two things you are comparing or contrasting?

✔ Do all sentences in the paragraph stay on topic?

ABOUT *SUPPORT*

✔ Have you compared or contrasted the subjects in at least three important ways?

✔ Have you provided specific details that effectively back up your supporting points?

ABOUT *COHERENCE*

✔ If you have chosen the point-by-point format, have you consistently discussed a point about one subject, then immediately discussed the same point about the other subject before moving on to the next point?

✔ If you have chosen the one-side-at-a-time format, have you discussed every point about one of your subjects, then discussed the same points *in the same order* about the second subjects?

✔ Have you used appropriate transitions, such as *first, in addition, also,* and *another way,* to help readers follow your train of thought?

ABOUT *SENTENCE SKILLS*

✔ Have you carefully proofread your paragraph, using the guidelines on the inside back cover of the book, and corrected all sentence-skills mistakes, including spelling?

Continue revising your work until you and your reader can answer *yes* to all these questions.

BEYOND THE CLASSROOM (Personal)

Comparison or Contrast

Imagine that a new club has opened in the building next to your house/apartment/dorm. At first, you were thrilled—but then loud music and screaming patrons started making it nearly impossible for you to study or sleep. Seven days a week, the club stays open until 2:00 A.M.

1. Write a paragraph-long letter of complaint to the club owners, contrasting life before and after the club opened.

2. Write an e-mail on the same topic to one of your friends.

3. How do the two pieces of writing (for two different purposes/audiences) differ from each other? How are they similar?

Definition

In talking with other people, we sometimes offer informal definitions to explain just what we mean by a particular term. Suppose, for example, we say to a friend, "Karen can be so clingy." We might then expand on our idea of "clingy" by saying, "You know, a clingy person needs to be with someone every single minute. If Karen's best friend makes plans that don't include her, she becomes hurt. And when she dates someone, she calls him several times a day and gets upset if he even goes to the grocery store without her. She hangs on to people too tightly." In a written definition, we make clear in a more complete and formal way our own personal understanding of a term. Such a definition typically starts with one meaning of a term. The meaning is then illustrated with a series of examples or a story.

A Paragraph to Consider

Active Learning

¹Active learning means more than just attending class—it requires students to be involved in their own education. ²Students who are active learners get ready for class by reading assignments ahead of time. ³However, instead of just sitting down, opening the text, reading the assigned pages, and then closing the book, active learners prepare and participate. ⁴Preparations could include gathering sticky notes, highlighter pens, pencils, and a computer. ⁵That computer is most often a laptop. ⁶Active learners then skim over the assignment, preparing the mind for what is going to be read. ⁷They read the text, use the sticky notes to mark areas that need clarification or sections that really stand out, and when they are done, quickly write or type a summary of the reading assignment. ⁸But active learners do far more than simply prepare well for class. ⁹Instead of passively sitting in the classroom, thinking about things they need to do, texting friends, or staring out the window, active learners take notes, ask questions, and write down ideas as they make personal and educational connections to what the instructor is saying. ¹⁰Once class is over, active learners don't promptly forget everything that was discussed. ¹¹Instead, active learners find time, immediately after class if possible or as soon as is feasible, to write down notes and ideas from the class that seemed important. ¹²Active learners also make time to meet with the instructor over the period of the course, not just to beg for mercy about grades, but to clarify ideas, get extra help, and have discussions to double-check understanding. ¹³Active learning means students take responsibility for learning and work to understand the material.

114   PART 2   Writing Effective Paragraphs

QUESTIONS

About Unity

1. Which sentence in "Active Learning" is irrelevant to the unity of the paragraph and should be eliminated? *(Write the sentence number here.)*

    _____

About Support

2. What three supporting points does the author provide to define active learning?

    _____

    _____

    _____

About Coherence

3. What are at least three transitions used within the "Active Learning" paragraph?

    _____   _____   _____   _____

Writing a Definition Paragraph

DEFINING A TV ADDICT

WRITING ASSIGNMENT

Academic

Write a paragraph that defines the term *TV addict*. Base your paragraph on the topic sentence and three supporting points provided below.

Topic sentence: Television addicts are people who will watch all the programs they can, for as long as they can, without doing anything else.

(1) TV addicts, first of all, will watch anything on the tube, no matter how bad it is. . . .

(2) In addition, addicts watch more hours of TV than normal people do. . . .

(3) Finally, addicts feel that TV is more important than other people or any other activities that might be going on. . . .

PREWRITING

a. Generate as many examples as you can for each of the three qualities of a TV addict. You can do this by asking yourself the following questions:

- What are some truly awful shows that I (or TV addicts I know) watch just because the television is turned on?

- What are some examples of the large amounts of time that I (or TV addicts I know) watch television?

DEFINE "GOOD."

Shoebox greeting card © Hallmark Cards, Kansas City.
Courtesy of Hallmark Cards, Inc.

RESPONDING TO IMAGES

Explain what makes this cartoon funny.

- What are some examples of ways that I (or TV addicts I know) neglect people or give up activities in order to watch TV?

    Write down every answer you can think of for each question. At this point, don't worry about writing full sentences or even about grammar or spelling. Just get your thoughts down on paper.

b. Look over the list of examples you have generated. Select the strongest examples you have thought of. You should have at least two or three for each quality. If not, ask yourself the questions in step *a* again.

c. Write out the examples you will use, this time expressing them in full, grammatically correct sentences.

d. Start with the topic sentence and three points provided in the assignment. Fill in the examples you've generated to support each point and write a first draft of your paragraph.

REVISING: PEER REVIEW

Put your first draft away for a day or so. When you come back to it, reread it critically and ask a friend or classmate to read it as well. The two of you should keep these questions in mind to make sure you have covered the four bases of effective writing:

CHECKLIST FOR DEFINITION: THE FOUR BASES

ABOUT *UNITY*

✔ Have you used the topic sentence and the three supporting points that were provided?

✔ Does every sentence in the paragraph help define the term *TV addict?*

ABOUT *SUPPORT*

✔ Have you backed up each supporting point with at least two examples?

✔ Does each of your examples effectively illustrate the point that it backs up?

ABOUT *COHERENCE*

✔ Have you used appropriate transitional language (*another, in addition, for example*) to tie your thoughts together?

✔ Are all transitional words correctly used?

ABOUT *SENTENCE SKILLS*

✔ Have you carefully proofread your paragraph, using the guidelines on the inside back cover of the book, and corrected all sentence-skills mistakes, including spelling?

✔ Have you used a consistent point of view throughout the paragraph?

Continue revising your work until you and your reader can answer *yes* to all these questions.

BEYOND THE CLASSROOM

Definition

Imagine that you are applying for a grant from your town or city government to build a community garden in an urban area or a community theater in a rural/suburban one. To make such an appeal effective, you will need to define *community*; such a definition will help you to show that the garden or theater will enhance the lives of everyone in this particular community. Use examples or one extended example to illustrate each of your general points.

Division-Classification

If you were doing the laundry, you might begin by separating the clothing into piles. You would then put all the whites in one pile and all the colors in another. Or you might classify the laundry, not according to color, but according to fabric—putting all cottons in one pile, polyesters in another, and so on. *Classifying* is the process of taking many things and separating them into categories. We generally classify to better manage or understand many things. Librarians classify books into groups (novels, travel, health, etc.) to make them easier to find. A scientist sheds light on the world by classifying all living things into two main groups: animals and plants.

Dividing, in contrast, is taking one thing and breaking it down into parts. We often divide, or analyze, to better understand, teach, or evaluate something. For instance, a tinkerer might take apart a clock to see how it works; a science text might divide a tree into its parts to explain their functions. A music reviewer may analyze the elements of a band's performance—for example, the skill of the various players, rapport with the audience, selections, and so on.

In short, if you are classifying, you are sorting *numbers of things* into categories. If you are dividing, you are breaking *one thing* into parts. It all depends on your purpose—you might classify flowers into various types or divide a single flower into its parts.

Two Paragraphs to Consider

Types of E-Mail

[1]As more and more people take advantage of e-mailing, three categories of e-mail have emerged. [2]One category of e-mail is junk mail. [3]When most people sign on to their computers, they are greeted with a flood of get-rich-quick schemes, invitations to pornographic Web sites, and ads for a variety of unwanted products. [4]E-mail users quickly become good at hitting the "delete" button to get rid of this garbage. [5]The second category that clogs most people's electronic mailbox is forwarded mail, most of which also gets deleted without being read. [6]The third and best category of e-mail is genuine personal e-mail from genuine personal friends. [7]Getting such real, thoughtful e-mail can almost make up for the irritation of the other two categories.

CHAPTER 4   Nine Patterns of Paragraph Development   117

Planning a Trip

[1]Designating a destination where the political and societal conditions are healthy and secure is the first and most important step in planning a trip. [2]Unstable governments very often lead to social unrest and violence. [3]Once settling on a general location, devising a budget is the next step. [4]The cost of living in some countries can be drastically higher than others. [5]When the destination is settled on, becoming familiar with the religious and cultural customs of the country is highly recommended. [6]What is accepted in the United States may be considered illegal or insulting in a foreign country. [7]For example, in Islamic countries, women are expected to cover their entire body and head. [8]In many instances, women wear veils across the face with a small slit positioned in front of the eyes. [9]Showing up in a tank top and shorts will very likely jeopardize one's sense of security and safety. [10]Now it is time to purchase an airline ticket and again, research is strongly advised in order to obtain the best possible deal. [11]Depending on one's idea of fun, planning an itinerary can be exceedingly complicated or relatively simple. [12]If lying on a lounge chair and sipping a cocktail by the water's edge is the desired activity, then planning the itinerary will be quite effortless. [13]But if a traveler is interested in involving himself or herself in some rigorous activities such as mountain climbing, scuba diving, or kayaking, planning the itinerary will probably require a lot more time. [14]Many people do not realize that there is in fact a lot of research involved in planning a trip. [15]These people should not be so careless, as they could expose themselves to extremely dangerous situations. [16]It is frustrating that so few people take research seriously.

About Unity

1. Which paragraph lacks a topic sentence?

   _____

2. Which sentence(s) in "Planning a Trip" should be eliminated in the interest of paragraph unity? *(Write the sentence number[s] here.)*

   _____

About Support

3. Which aspect of "Planning a Trip" lacks specific details?

   _____

4. After which sentence in "Types of E-Mail" are supporting details needed? *(Write the sentence number here.)*

   _____

118   PART 2   Writing Effective Paragraphs

About Coherence

5. Which paragraph uses emphatic order to organize its details?

_____

6. Which words in "Types of E-mail" signal the most important detail?

_____

Writing a Division-Classification Paragraph

ORGANIZING CATEGORIES

Below are four options to develop into a classification paragraph. Each one presents a topic to classify into three categories. Choose one option to develop into a paragraph.

OPTION 1
Books
(1) Classics
(2) Best sellers
(3) Beach reads

OPTION 2
Movies
(1) Action
(2) Comedy
(3) Horror

OPTION 3
Responsibilities
(1) Family
(2) School
(3) Work

OPTION 4
House pets
(1) Dogs
(2) Cats
(3) Birds

PREWRITING

a. Begin by doing some freewriting on the topic you have chosen. For five or ten minutes, simply write down everything that comes into your head when you think about "books," "house pets," or whichever option you choose. Don't worry about grammar, spelling, or organization—just write.

b. Now that you've "loosened up your brain" a little, try asking yourself questions about the topic and writing down your answers. If you are writing about house pets, for instance, you might ask questions like these:

• What are some unique qualities for each kind of house pet?

• How do these house pets differ? How are they similar?

• What would dog owners say about their dogs? What would cat owners say about their cats? What would bird owners say about their birds?

Write down whatever answers occur to you for these and other questions. Again, do not worry at this stage about writing correctly. Instead, concentrate on getting down all the information you can think of that supports your three points.

c.   Reread the material you have accumulated. If some of the details you have written make you think of even better ones, add them. Select the details that best support your three points. Number them in the order you will present them.

d.   Restate your topic as a grammatically complete topic sentence. For example, if you're writing about responsibilities, your topic sentence might be "Responsibilities can be divided into three categories." Turn each of your three supporting points into a full sentence as well.

e.   Using your topic sentence and three supporting sentences and adding the details you have generated, write the first draft of your paragraph.

REVISING: PEER REVIEW

Put your work away for a couple of days. Then reread it with a critical eye and have a friend or classmate read it as well. Ask your reader to give you honest feedback as the two of you answer the following questions.

CHECKLIST FOR DIVISION-CLASSIFICATION: THE FOUR BASES

ABOUT *UNITY*

✔   Does the paragraph include a complete topic sentence and three supporting points?

ABOUT *SUPPORT*

✔   Have you backed up each supporting point with strong, specific details?

ABOUT *COHERENCE*

✔   Does the paragraph successfully classify types of books, movies, responsibilities, or house pets?

ABOUT *SENTENCE SKILLS*

✔   Have you carefully proofread the paragraph, using the list on the inside back cover of the book, and corrected all sentence-skills mistakes, including spelling?

✔   Have you used specific rather than general words?

Continue revising your work until you and your reader can answer *yes* to all these questions.

Imagine that you are a real estate agent and someone new to the area has asked you for suggestions about where to look for a home. Write a paragraph classifying local neighborhoods into three or more types. For each type, include an explanation with one or more examples.

BEYOND THE CLASSROOM   Work

Division-Classification

Argument

Most of us know someone who enjoys a good argument. Such a person usually challenges any sweeping statement we might make. "Why do you say that?" he or she will ask. "Give your reasons." Our questioner then listens carefully as we cite our reasons, waiting to see if we really do have solid evidence to support our point of view. In an argument, the two parties each present their supporting evidence. The goal is to determine who has the more solid evidence to support his or her point of view. A questioner may make us feel a bit nervous, but we may also appreciate the way he or she makes us think through our opinions.

The ability to advance sound, compelling arguments is an important skill in everyday life. We can use argument to get an extension on a term paper, obtain a favor from a friend, or convince an employer that we are the right person for a job. Understanding persuasion based on clear, logical reasoning can also help us see through the sometimes faulty arguments advanced by advertisers, editors, politicians, and others who try to bring us over to their side.

A Paragraph to Consider

Living Alone

[1]Living alone is quite an experience. [2]People who live alone, for one thing, have to learn to do all kinds of tasks by themselves. [3]They must learn—even if they have had no experience—to change fuses, put up curtains and shades, temporarily dam an overflowing toilet, cook a meal, and defrost a refrigerator. [4]When there is no father, husband, mother, or wife to depend on, a person can't fall back on the excuse, "I don't know how to do that." [5]Those who live alone also need the strength to deal with people. [6]Alone, singles must face noisy neighbors, unresponsive landlords, dishonest repair people, and aggressive bill collectors. [7]Because there are no buffers between themselves and the outside world, people living alone have to handle every visitor—friendly or unfriendly—alone. [8]Finally, singles need a large dose of courage to cope with occasional panic and unavoidable loneliness. [9]That weird thump in the night is even more terrifying when there is no one in the next bed or the next room. [10]Frightening weather or unexpected bad news is doubly bad when the worry can't be shared. [11]Even when life is going well, little moments of sudden loneliness can send shivers through the heart. [12]Struggling through such bad times taps into reserves of courage that people may not have known they possessed. [13]Facing everyday tasks, confronting all types of people, and handling panic and loneliness can shape singles into brave, resourceful, and more independent people.

CHAPTER 4 Nine Patterns of Paragraph Development 121

About Unity

1. The topic sentence in "Living Alone" is too broad. Circle the topic sentence that states accurately what the paragraph is about.

    a. Living alone can make one a better person.

    b. Living alone can create feelings of loneliness.

    c. Living alone should be avoided.

2. How many reasons are given to support the topic sentence in this paragraph?

    _____ one _____ two _____ three _____ four

About Coherence

3. What are the three main transition words in this paragraph?

    _____ _____ _____

Writing an Argument Paragraph

SUPPORTING A POSITION

Develop an argument paragraph based on one of these statements:

Students should (*or* should not) be held back in school if they fail a class.

_____ (*name a specific athlete*) is the athlete most worthy of admiration in his *or* her sport.

Television is one of the best (*or* worst) inventions of this century.

_____ make the best (*or* worst) pets.

Students should (*or* should not) take a year off between high school and college.

Teenagers make poor parents.

_____ is one public figure today who can be considered a hero.

This college needs a better _____ (cafeteria *or* library *or* student center *or* grading policy *or* attendance policy).

PREWRITING

a. Make up brief outlines for any three of the preceding statements. Make sure you have three separate and distinct reasons for each statement. Below is an example of a brief outline for a paragraph making another point.

Large cities should outlaw passenger cars.

1. Cut down on smog and pollution

2. Cut down on noise

3. Make more room for pedestrians

b. Decide, perhaps through discussion with your instructor or classmates, which of your outlines is the most promising for development into a paragraph. Make sure your supporting points are logical by asking yourself in each case, "Does this item truly support my topic sentence?"

c. Do some prewriting. Prepare a list of all the details you can think of that might actually support your point. Don't limit yourself; include more details than you can actually use. Here, for example, are details generated by the writer of "Living Alone":

Deal with power failures	Noisy neighbors
Nasty landlords	Develop courage
Scary noises at night	Do all the cooking
Spiders	Home repairs
Bill collectors	Obscene phone calls
Frightening storms	Loneliness

d. Decide which details you will use to develop your paragraph. Number the details in the order in which you will present them. Because presenting the strongest reason last (emphatic order) is the most effective way to organize an argument paragraph, be sure to save your most powerful reason for last. Here is how the author of "Living Alone" made decisions about details:

1. Deal with power failures
4. Nasty landlords
7. Scary noises at night
   ~~Spiders~~
6. Bill collectors
8. Frightening storms
5. Noisy neighbors
10. Develop courage
2. Do all the cooking
3. Home repairs
   ~~Obscene phone calls~~
9. Loneliness

e. Write the first draft of your paragraph. As you write, develop each reason with specific details. For example, in "Living Alone," notice how the writer makes the experience of living alone come alive with phrases like "That weird thump in the night" or "little moments of sudden loneliness can send shivers through the heart."

REVISING: PEER REVIEW

Put your paragraph away for a day or so. Then, share your paragraph with a partner and refer to the following questions to make sure you have covered the four bases of effective writing:

CHECKLIST FOR ARGUMENT: THE FOUR BASES

ABOUT *UNITY*

✔ Imagine that your audience is a jury who will ultimately render a verdict on your argument. Have you presented a convincing case? If you were on the jury, would you both understand and be favorably impressed by this argument?

✔ Does every one of your supporting points help prove the argument stated in your topic sentence?

ABOUT *SUPPORT*

✔ Have you backed up your points of support with specific details?

✔ Have you appealed to your readers' senses with these details?

ABOUT *COHERENCE*

✔ Have you used emphatic order in your paragraph, saving the most important, strongest detail for last?

ABOUT *SENTENCE SKILLS*

✔ Have you used strong verbs (rather than *is* and *to be*) throughout?

✔ Have you written your argument in the active, rather than passive, voice? (see pages 424–437)

✔ Have you checked your paper for sentence-skills mistakes, including spelling?

Continue revising your work until you and your partner can answer *yes* to all these questions.

Imagine that you have implemented a new procedure at work, one that will make your workplace more efficient. For example, if you work at a retail store, you may have reorganized the customer files by zip code rather than by last name. Write a one-paragraph memo to your supervisor explaining in detail why you chose to implement this procedure and why he or she would approve or endorse this change. Do your best to convince your supervisor that your idea brings more efficiency.

BEYOND THE CLASSROOM

Argument

124   PART 2   Writing Effective Paragraphs

REFLECTIVE ACTIVITY

1. Reread two or three paragraphs you have written in response to the writing assignments in this chapter. Are these paragraphs unified? Do any contain off-target sentences?

2. Are the paragraphs coherent, or do you need to add transitions? Which ones?

3. Does each paragraph contain enough support?

EXPLORING WRITING ONLINE

Examine your college's home page and consider what patterns of development it uses—and for what purposes. In your response, consider some of the following questions: How does the home page describe and/or define your school, and does it serve to narrate your college's story? As a prospective student, what kind of first impression does this page (not the site as a whole) offer? How is it an *argument* or advertisement for you school? How does it use *classification* and/or *division* as organizing principles? Does the site seem easy to navigate? What might you, as a current student, use the site for?

RESPONDING TO IMAGES

The following images address the topic of same-sex marriage. Why do you think the photographs were taken? Consider issues of purpose and audience. What patterns of development are at work in each image? How might the reason a photograph is taken differ from how it is used in a textbook?

PART **2**

CHAPTER **1**

ESL Students

Simple Sentences

Quick Facts ESL Students

- Every day, English is spoken by more people as a second language than as a native language.

- Millions of people all over the world study English as a foreign language.

- International students at colleges and universities:
  Canada: 60,000 (1994)   U.S.: 450,000 (1995)

- Average number of immigrants and refugees who came to North America each year from 1990–1995:
  Canada: 215,000   U.S.: 900,000

- Percentage of people in the U.S. over five years old who reported speaking a language other than English at home:
  6.2 percent (1990)

- Percentage of people in Canada who reported speaking a language other than English or French at home:
  7 percent (1991)

Words to Know

ESL   (English as a Second Language) Studying English if English is not your native language. Sometimes this also means you are studying in a country that uses English.

EFL   (English as a Foreign Language) Studying English in a country that does not use English as a native or official language.

international student   A person who comes to another country to study and then returns to his or her country.

immigrant   A person who comes to another country to live permanently.

refugee   A person who comes to another country because of war or danger in his or her home country.

ESOL   (English for Speakers of Other Languages) This term is often used for both ESL and EFL situations.

And You?

Are you studying ESL or EFL?

If you are an ESL student, are you an international student, immigrant, or refugee?

What are your reasons for studying English?

Form

A simple sentence has at least one subject and one full verb and tells a complete thought. It consists of one independent clause.

Simple sentences look like this:

```
                    S V
           S and  S V
        S, S, and  S V
                    S V   or V
                    S V   and V
                    S V,  V, and V
           S and  S V   and V
        S, S, and  S V   and V
```

Simple sentences can be very short.

```
      S   V
Chan is an immigrant.
```

Simple sentences can also be long.

```
     S                                    V
The tall young man with dark hair and glasses speaks nearly fluent English.
```

Example Sentences

The following sentences are simple sentences about students in an ESL class. Note the subjects and verb in each sentence.

```
   S   V
```
1. Tariq is an ESL student.

```
   S   V
```
2. Kim came to Canada three years ago.

```
   S   V
```
3. Li wants to be an English teacher.
   Note: to be is the object in this sentence. It is not a verb.

```
    S    V
```
4. Teresa loves living in a foreign country.
   Note: living is the object in this sentence. It is not a verb.

```
    S      hv   V
```
5. ESL students should try to speak with native speakers.

```
    V
```
6. Study hard!
   Note: The subject you is understood in commands.

PART **2** WRITING FOCUS

Simple sentences may have more than one subject and more than one verb, but the subjects are together and the verbs are together. They are connected with *and* or *or*.

         S   S   V

7. Canada and the U.S. have many immigrants.

        S   S   S   hv   V

8. Immigrants, refugees, and international students may study together in one class.

   Note: Three or more items in a list (subjects or verbs) need commas. The comma before *and* is preferred, but not necessary.

           S   hv   V   V

9. Next year, Stephan will study at a college or get a job.

   Note: You do not need to repeat the helping verb *will* with the second verb *get*.

                  S   V   V

10. Every day after class, Young Sil practices her speaking and does her homework with a study group.

        S   V   V   V

11. Chang immigrated to Los Angeles, got a job, and now owns his own company.

       S   S   V   V

12. Irina and Sarah study English and run a day-care.

Be sure you write a complete sentence with a subject and a verb. Note the following incomplete sentences, called fragments.

See Fragments on page 93 for more information and practice.

(A) Make sure you have a verb in the sentence.

          S

No: English a very difficult subject.

          S   V

Yes: English is a very difficult subject.

          S

No: My school far away.

          S   V

Yes: My school is far away.

B In formal writing, words such as *because, if, although,* and *when* cannot begin a simple sentence. They are used in complex sentences.

See Adverb Clauses on page 53 for more information.

                      S V

No: Although I'm homesick.

                  S V

Yes: I'm homesick.

                    s v   S V

Yes: Although I'm homesick, I will stay here for two years.

C If you use *for example* and *such as*, make sure you have a subject and a verb in the sentence.

No: For example, San Francisco.

                          S   V

Yes: For example, San Francisco has many Chinese immigrants.

No: Such as Ukraine.

                       S   V

Yes: Many recent immigrants come from Eastern European countries, such as Ukraine.

Sentence Practice

Exercise 1

Write **S** above the subject(s) and **V** above the verb(s).

Studying English as a Second Language

1. Many ESL students come to the United States and Canada to start a new life.

2. Other ESL students come to North America to study English and other subjects.

3. Most ESL students enjoy getting to know students from around the world.

4. Yumiko, Abdullah, and Kwang Ho are ESL students at North City Community College.

5. They are studying English and taking other college classes.

6. Hwang and Christine take classes and work full-time.

Exercise 2

Write S above the subject(s) and V above the verb(s). Then write SS in the blank if the sentence is a simple sentence or F if the sentence is a fragment (incomplete sentence).

Studying English as a Foreign Language

1. _____ Thousands of students all over the world study English in their

   own countries.

2. _____ Because English has become an international language.

3. _____ When people study English in a non-English-speaking country.

4. _____ It is sometimes called English as a Foreign Language, or EFL.

5. _____ Elementary students, junior high students, and high school

   students often take English in school as a required subject.

6. _____ Some EFL students take special English classes to help them pass

   a test.

7. _____ Such as a college entrance exam or the TOEFL* test.

8. _____ English a very popular language nowadays.

---

* Test of English as a Foreign Language

Exercise 3

On another piece of paper, write a paragraph by combining each group of sentences into one simple sentence. Use *and* or *or*. Think carefully about commas. Your paragraph should have six sentences.

ESL Students

1. Thousands of ESL students live in North America.

   Thousands of ESL students study English at high schools, colleges, and universities.

2. International students study ESL to improve their lives.

   Immigrants study ESL to improve their lives.

   Refugees study ESL to improve their lives.

3. Many international students work on ESL first.

   Many international students take regular college classes later.

4. International students take classes for fun.

   International students study for college degrees.

   International students improve their English for their profession.

5. Immigrants study ESL to survive in an English-speaking country.

   Immigrants study ESL to take college classes.

   Immigrants study ESL to get good jobs.

   Refugees study ESL to survive in an English-speaking country.

   Refugees study ESL to take college classes.

   Refugees study ESL to get good jobs.

6. They often study ESL.

   They often have a job.

   They often take care of their families.

Writing Practice (Optional)

Ten Perfect Sentences   To practice writing simple sentences and to practice editing carefully for grammar problems, you will write ten perfect simple sentences. Your teacher may ask you to write about students in your class or about another topic that he or she chooses.

a. Your sentences must be the type of sentences you are practicing, for example, simple sentences. The punctuation must be correct. All additional grammar points must be correct.

b. Try a variety of types of simple sentences (SSV, SVV, etc.). Check the sentences very carefully for correct grammar, punctuation, spelling, and expression. It is important to write and check these sentences by yourself.

c. Your teacher will check your sentences and circle the number of the correct sentences. Congratulations!

d. If a sentence has any problems or is not a simple sentence, your teacher will make the corrections in the sentence.

e. Then your teacher (or you) can count the number of correct sentences. If you wrote ten perfect simple sentences, great! You are finished with this exercise. You can work on self-study. If you didn't write ten perfect sentences, you need to write new (different) sentences until you have a total of ten perfect sentences.

This is more difficult than you think! It may take you several tries. Keep working on your sentences until you are finished.

The student sample that follows will help you understand.

Here is an example of a student's Ten Perfect Sentences. This student wrote sentences about her family.

Ten Perfect Simple Sentences

1. My f/father work^s at_a computer factory.

2. My m/Mother/ she stay^s and work^s at home.

3. My sister is studying in high school.

4. My grandmother and my grandfather live with my aunt and help with her children.

5. I love and respec^t my parent^s.

6. If you will meet my family, you will like them.   **(Not a simple sentence)**

7. My brother/ he is only six year^s old.

8. Sometime^s I play with my brother and cousin.

9. My sister or I make dinner every Saturday.

10. I always help my mother in the kitchen.

6 more

(Note that the student wrote four perfect simple sentences. She needed to write six more sentences. They must be different sentences. First, she looked at her old sentences to see what mistakes she had. Then, on the same piece of paper, she wrote six new sentences.)

1. My family and I came to the United State^s three years ago.

2. My father plays piano and likes to read.

3. My sister likes (very much) her friends and her classmates.

4. I have many cousins.

5. Some of the my cousins live in the United State.

6. My brother and his friend are on a soccer team.

3 more

(She wrote three more.)

1. My sister and her friends like to go roller-blading.

2. I live together with my family in a little house.

3. My mother likes to read and sew.

OK

(She finished Ten Perfect Sentences.)

Writing Topics

Your teacher may ask you to write a paragraph or essay on one of the following topics:

1. Interview another student in your class. Write about his or her life and/or future plans.

   (Narration)

2. Describe an English as a Second Language class or an English as a Foreign Language class you have had. Write about the teacher, students, and activities in class.

   (Description)

3. What are your reasons for studying English? How will knowing more English benefit you?

   (Reasons)

Answer Key to Chapter 1   Simple Sentences

Exercise 1

                S   V
1. Many ESL students come to the United States and Canada to start a new life.

              S   V
2. Other ESL students come to North America to study English and other subjects.

              S   V
3. Most ESL students enjoy getting to know students from around the world.

      S   S   S   V
4. Yumiko, Abdullah, and Kwang Ho are ESL students at North City Community College.

      S hv V   V
5. They are studying English and taking other college classes.

      S   S   V   V
6. Hwang and Christine take classes and work full-time.

Exercise 2

                         S   V
1. __SS__ Thousands of students all over the world study English in their own countries.

                 S hv V
2. __F__ Because English has become an international language.

               S   V
3. __F__ When people study English in a non-English-speaking country.

              S hv   V
4. __SS__ It is sometimes called English as a Foreign Language, or EFL.

                     S   S
5. __SS__ Elementary students, junior high students, and high school

               S   V
        students often take English in school as a required subject.

                    S   V
6. __SS__ Some EFL students take special English classes to help them pass a test.

7. __F__ Such as a college entrance exam or the TOEFL test.

                 S
8. __F__ English a very popular language nowadays.

Answer Key to Chapter 1 — Simple Sentences

(Concluded)

Exercise 3

Best answer:

Thousands of ESL students live in North America <u>and</u> study English at high schools, colleges, and universities. International students, immigrants, <u>and</u> refugees study ESL to improve their lives. Many international students work on ESL first <u>and</u> take regular college classes later. International students take classes for fun, study for college degrees, <u>or</u> to improve their English for their profession. Immigrants <u>and</u> refugees study ESL to survive in an English-speaking country, to take college classes, or* to get good jobs. They often study ESL, have a job, <u>and</u> take care of their families.

* *and* could be used here, but *or* is a better answer because most students takes classes for one of those reasons, not for all of them.

Note: The commas are optional before connecting words in lists of three or more.

PART **2**

CHAPTER **2**

Siblings

Less Formal Compound Sentences

Quick Facts   Siblings

- Average family size: U.S.: 3.19   Canada: 2.9
- Average number of children per mother: U.S.: 2.06   Canada: 1.81
- The number of twins, triplets, and other multiple births has tripled since 1990 due to older women having babies and to fertility treatments. Twenty-five percent of the women who receive fertility treatments to help them become pregnant have more than one child (twins, triplets, quadruplets, quintuplets).
- The largest number of children born at one time to one mother: 10

- The birth order of some famous people:

  First-born: Rock singer Courtney Love, Presidents Bill Clinton and George Washington, Chinese Leader Mao Tse Tung

  Middle-born: Civil Rights Leader Martin Luther King, Jr., Cuban Leader Fidel Castro, actor Michael J. Fox, President Richard Nixon, journalist Barbara Walters

  Last-born: Indian Leader Mahatma Gandhi, actor Eddie Murphy, actress Goldie Hawn

  Only child: Artist Leonardo da Vinci, singer Elvis Presley, model Brooke Shields

Words to Know

sibling   Brother or sister.

twins   Two children born to the same mother at the same time.

triplets   Three children born to the same mother at the same time.

quadruplets   Four children born to the same mother at the same time.

quintuplets   Five children born to the same mother at the same time.

And You?

- How many siblings do you have?

  Are you a first-born, middle-born, youngest, or only child?

  Are there twins, triplets, or other multiple-birth children in your family?

Form

Compound sentences are two simple sentences (two "independent clauses") that are joined together because of their meaning. There can be more than one subject or more than one verb in the simple sentence. This chapter discusses less formal compound sentences with connecting words like *and, but, or*, and *so*.

Note: Connecting words are sometimes called *coordinating conjunctions*.

Less formal compound sentences look like this:

S V	, connecting word	S V
SENTENCE		SENTENCE
	, and	
	, but	
	, or	
	, so	

The two sentences have equal importance.

Note: Compound sentences need a comma after the first simple sentence unless the sentences are very short.

Example Sentences

The following sentences are informal compound sentences about two sisters. Note the subjects and verbs in each sentence and the meaning of the connecting words.

S = subject
V = verb
hv = helping verb
cw = connecting word

Very common connecting words: *and, but, or, so.*

    S V   cw S V
1. Terri has twins, and Beth has triplets.
   Note: and shows a similarity.

    S   V   cw S V
2. They both love their children, but they have questions about raising them.
   Note: but shows a difference.

    S hv V   S hv V
3. Beth will stay home with the children, or she will go back to work.
   Note: or shows a choice and is often in the future.

    S   V   cw S V
4. They wanted to find others with twins or triplets, so they formed a parents' group.
   Note: so shows a result.

Less common connecting words: *for, yet, nor.* *

                   S   V   cw   S   V

5. Terri's twins aren't identical, yet people still have trouble telling them apart.

Note: yet shows a difference. It is like *but* only more formal.

                 S   hv   V   cw   S   V

6. Terri's twins don't dress alike, for they want to be different.

Note: for shows a reason and means *because.*

                 S   hv   V   cw hv S V

7. Terri's twins don't look exactly alike, nor do they act alike.

* *Note:* **nor** is a very unusual connecting word. It means "not this and not that." After *nor,* the word order is like a question.

Watch Out For...

A In very formal English, do not begin a sentence with a connecting word. In informal writing, it is usually OK to begin a sentence with a connecting word, but not too often.

No: And my mother is an only child.

Yes: My father is the youngest child in his family, and my mother is an only child.

No: But, my roommate comes from a large family.

Yes: I come from a small family, but my roommate comes from a large family.

No: So she used fertility drugs.

Yes: Pat couldn't have children, so she used fertility drugs.

No: Or, I may have triplets.

Yes: The doctors think I will have twins, or I may have triplets.

B In written English, you cannot begin a line with a comma. Put it at the end of the line instead.

No: Thomas is interested in sports

       , but his twin brother prefers reading.

Yes: Thomas is interested in sports,

       but his twin brother prefers reading.

C The words *also* and *then* are not connecting words. You need more than a comma (a period or a semicolon) to use them between sentences.

No: My brothers fought as children, then they were friends later.

Yes: My brothers fought as children. Then they were friends later.

No: My brothers share many interests, they also look alike.

Yes: My brothers share many interests; they also look alike.

Sentence Practice

Exercise 1

Write **S** over the subjects and **V** over the verbs in the following compound sentences.

Twins

1. Twins are two children born to the same mother at the same time, and there are two types of twins.

2. Identical twins are from one egg, but fraternal twins are from two eggs.

3. Identical twins have the same blood type, and they also have identical fingerprints.

4. Some identical twins look almost exactly alike, so it can be very difficult to tell them apart.

5. Identical twins are always the same sex, but fraternal twins can be the same or different sex.

6. Fraternal twins can be two girls or two boys, or they can be a girl and a boy.

7. Fraternal twins may not look very much alike, for they are actually the same as other sisters or brothers.

Exercise 2

Mark S over the subjects and V over the verbs in the following sentences. Then decide if they are simple or compound sentences. In the blanks, write SS for a simple sentence and CS for a compound sentence. Add commas to the compound sentences. The first sentence is done for you.

Birth Order

1. __CS__   Psychologists have studied children according to their birth order,
   and they have discovered the following general results.

2. _____   First-born children often have strong personalities and like
   to be leaders.

3. _____   They usually get high grades in school but they also get angry
   more easily than other children.

4. _____   Middle children are usually satisfied with their place in the family
   and they are quite flexible.

5. _____   Middle children generally follow the rules so they don't get into
   trouble very much.

6. _____   The youngest children in the family like to get along with other
   people and to try new things.

7. _____   Only children often need their parents but they are also
   self-confident.

8. _____   These descriptions may fit your family well or they may not
   describe the children in your family.

9. _____   Each family is different so no description of birth order is perfect.

Exercise 3

On another piece of paper, combine each pair of sentences into one simple or compound sentence. Use *and, but, or, so,* or *for*. Be sure to use commas correctly.

Quadruplets

1. Christine and Lyle wanted to have another baby.

    Christine was not able to get pregnant.

2. She had an operation to help her get pregnant.

    It worked.

3. Seven months later, Christine gave birth to quadruplets.

    Aili, Daisey, Max, and Nathan joined the family.

4. At first, Christine panicked at the babies' crying.

    After a few months, she learned to help one and say "just a minute" to the others.

5. Having four babies is a lot of work.

    Christine has learned to ask for help from friends and neighbors.

6. Nine-year-old brother Benjamin is good at changing diapers.

    He likes making faces at the babies and watching them smile.

Writing Practice (Optional)

Write Ten Perfect Compound Sentences. Use each of the common connecting words, and be sure that they make sense for the meaning of the sentence. Check carefully for commas and other grammar and punctuation. You may want to write about your family or about another topic your teacher suggests. *(See pages 30–32 for instructions and an example.)*

Writing Topics

Your teacher may ask you to write a paragraph or essay on one of the following topics:

1. If you have siblings, describe how they are similar or different from you or from each other (or describe two siblings you know well). If you have more than one child, discuss how they are similar or different.

   (Comparison / Contrast)

2. Are you a first-born, middle-born, youngest, or only child? Do you fit the descriptions given in Exercise 2? Why or why not?

   (Reasons)

3. Discuss the advantages and disadvantages of being an only child or coming from a large family. You can write from your own experience or the experience of others.

   (Advantages / Disadvantages)

Answer Key to Chapter 2   Less Formal Compound Sentences

Exercise 1

              S   V

1. Twins are two children born to the same mother at the same time, and

      S   V

there are two types of twins.

            S   V   S   V

2. Identical twins are from one egg, but fraternal twins are from two eggs.

           S   V   S   V

3. Identical twins have the same blood type, and they also have identical
fingerprints.

          S   V   S (hv) V

4. Some identical twins look almost exactly alike, so it can be very difficult to
tell them apart.

          S   V   S (hv) V

5. Identical twins are always the same sex, but fraternal twins can be the
same or different sex.

          S (hv) V   S (hv) V

6. Fraternal twins can be two girls or two boys, or they can be a girl
and a boy.

          S   (hv) V   S   V

7. Fraternal twins may not look very much alike, for they are actually the
same as other sisters or brothers.

Exercise 2

                S   (hv)   V

1. __CS__ Psychologists have studied children according to their birth order,

          S (hv)   V

and they have discovered the following general results.

                S   V   V

2. __SS__ First-born children often have strong personalities and like
to be leaders.

              S   V   S   V

3. __CS__ They usually get high grades in school, but they also get angry
more easily than other children.

              S   V

4. __CS__ Middle children are usually satisfied with their place in the family,

          S   V

and they are quite flexible.

              S   V   S (hv) V

5. __CS__ Middle children generally follow the rules, so they don't get into
trouble very much.

Answer Key to Chapter 2   Less Formal Compound Sentences

(Concluded)

6. __SS__ The youngest children in the family like to get along with other people and to try new things.

7. __CS__ Only children often need their parents, but they are also self-confident.

8. __CS__ These descriptions may fit your family well, or they may not describe the children in your family.

9. __CS__ Each family is different, so no description of birth order is perfect.

Exercise 3

Suggested answer:

Christine and Lyle wanted to have another baby, <u>but</u> Christine was not able to get pregnant. She had an operation to help her get pregnant, <u>and</u> it worked. Seven months later, Christine gave birth to quadruplets, <u>and</u> / <u>so</u> Aili, Daisey, Max, and Nathan joined the family. At first, Christine panicked at the babies' crying, <u>but</u> after a few months, she learned to help one and say "just a minute" to the others. Having four babies is a lot of work, <u>so</u> / <u>but</u> Christine has learned to ask for help from friends and neighbors. Nine-year-old brother Benjamin is good at changing diapers, <u>and</u> / <u>for</u> he likes making faces at the babies and watching them smile.

PART **2**

CHAPTER **3**

Holidays

More Formal Compound Sentences

Quick Facts **Holidays**

■ Even though the same holidays are observed in many different countries around the world, there is a variety of ways in which people celebrate them.

■ Here are the main holidays in Canada and the United States:

Canada		United States	
New Year's Day*	January 1st	New Year's Day*	January 1st
		Martin Luther King Day*	3rd Monday in January
Valentine's Day	February 14th	Valentine's Day	February 14th
Easter Sunday	late March or early April	Presidents' Day*	3rd Monday in February
Easter Monday	Monday after Easter	Easter Sunday	late March or early April
Victoria Day*	3rd Monday in May	Memorial Day*	last Monday in May
Canada Day*	July 1st	Independence Day*	July 4th
Labour Day*	1st Monday in September	Labor Day*	1st Monday in September
Halloween	October 31st	Halloween	October 31st
Thanksgiving Day*	2nd Monday in October	Veterans Day	November 11th
Remembrance Day*	November 11th	Thanksgiving Day*	4th Thursday in November
Christmas Day*	December 25th	Christmas Day*	December 25th
Boxing Day*	December 26th		

* National holiday: most government offices and schools are closed.

And You?

● Of the holidays above or of holidays in your native culture, what is your favorite holiday? Why?

What is your least favorite holiday? Why?

Form

In this chapter you will study compound sentences that use a semicolon (;) and usually a transition word (sometimes called a "conjunctive adverb"). These sentences are very similar to compound sentences with connecting words, but they are more formal.

More formal compound sentences look like this:

```
   S       V        ; transition word,      S        V
(SENTENCE                                SENTENCE)
```

```
              ; in addition,
              ; moreover,        (similar meaning to and)
              ; furthermore,

              ; however,         (similar meaning to but)
              ; nevertheless,

              ; otherwise,       (or + result)

              ; therefore,
              ; consequently,    (similar meaning to so)
              ; as a result,
```

Compound sentences can also look like this:

```
   S       V        ;        S        V
(SENTENCE           ;     SENTENCE)
```

Example Sentences

Transition words are often used at the beginning of a sentence. They are usually simple sentences. The transition word introduces the second sentence.

> My family always gets together with our relatives at Christmas. In addition, we have a big family picnic on the Fourth of July.

If the connection between the two sentences is very strong, the writer may want to combine the sentences together with a semicolon and a transition word. Here are compound sentences about holidays. Note the subjects, verbs, and transition words in each sentence.

S = subject
V = verb
hv = helping verb
trans = transition word

          S   V
1. On Independence Day, Americans meet with their friends and family for

                    trans   S   V
barbecues and picnics; in addition, most cities have big fireworks displays.

Note: The transition words *in addition, furthermore,* and *moreover* show similarity, almost the same as *and*. Often the idea in the second part of the sentence is stronger than in the first.

  S

2. On some holidays, such as Veteran's Day and President's Day, all banks,

      S   S hv V   **trans**

schools, and U.S. government offices are closed; however, most private

      S   S   V

offices and stores remain open.

Note: The transition words *however* and *nevertheless* show difference or unexpected result. They mean almost the same as *but.*

 S V   **trans**   S hv V

3. It's good to know about Halloween; otherwise, you will be surprised by
people in strange costumes.
Note: The transition word *otherwise* means *if not + result.* It is similar to *or* plus a result.

                    S   V

4. Many Americans wanted to make a day to celebrate the life of

                         trans   S hv

Martin Luther King, Jr.; therefore, Martin Luther King Day was

      V

established in 1989.

Note: The transition words *therefore, consequently,* and *as a result* show a result. They mean almost the same as *so.*

If sentences are closely related, only a semicolon can be used. This is possible, but less common in English.

                              S   V   V

5. On New Year's Eve, many people go to parties and stay up

               S   V

until midnight; they like to greet the New Year with friends.

Watch Out For...

A) If there is no punctuation between two complete sentences, it is a run-on sentence. *See Run-ons on page 105 for more information.*

                            S V   S   V

No: In Canada, July first is Canada Day the first Monday in August is Civic Holiday in some areas.

B) Two complete sentences cannot be joined by only a comma. This is called a comma splice. *See Comma Splice on page 113 for more information.*

                            S V   S   V

No: In Canada, July first is Canada Day, the first Monday in August is Civic Holiday in some areas.

There are many ways to fix run-on and comma splice sentences:

Yes: In Canada, July first is Canada Day, and the first Monday in August is Civic Holiday in some areas.

Yes: In Canada, July first is Canada Day; in addition, the first Monday in August is Civic Holiday in some areas.

Yes: In Canada, July first is Canada Day. In addition, the first Monday in August is Civic Holiday in some areas.

Yes: In Canada, July first is Canada Day. The first Monday in August is Civic Holiday in some areas.

Yes: In Canada, July first is Canada Day; the first Monday in August is Civic Holiday in some areas.

Sentence Practice

Exercise 1

Write S over the subject(s) and V over the verb(s). Then write *and, but, so,* or *or* above the transition word to show its meaning. The first sentence is done for you.

Thanksgiving

    S   V   **and** S
Americans have a Thanksgiving holiday every fall; in addition, Canadians
  V
celebrate Thanksgiving in the fall. Canadians celebrate Thanksgiving on the

second Monday in October; however, in the U.S. Thanksgiving is celebrated

on the fourth Thursday in November. Long ago, the early European settlers

survived a hard winter and had successful crops; therefore, they prepared a

big meal together with their Indian neighbors and friends to thank God.

Nowadays, people in both countries get together with their families and

friends to eat a big dinner with traditional foods, such as turkey, potatoes,

and pumpkin pie; moreover, they use this day to express their thankfulness

for life. On Thanksgiving Day, we should not eat too much; otherwise, we

may feel sick.

Exercise 2

Write **S** over the subject(s) and **V** over the verb(s) in the following simple and compound sentences. Then write **C** in the blank if the sentence is correct. Write **I** if there is any mistake in punctuation and change the sentence to make it correct. The first sentence is done for you.

May Day

$$\text{S} \quad \text{V} \qquad\qquad\qquad \text{S} \quad \text{V}$$

1. __C__   May 1st is a holiday in many countries; it is a day for workers.

2. _____   May 1st is a big holiday in Europe however in North America,

Labor Day is in September.

3. _____   May 1st in the U.S. is called "May Day," and it is a kind of

celebration for spring.

4. _____   In the past, children danced around a Maypole on this day,

moreover, people made May flower baskets to bring to

their neighbors.

5. _____   Usually a child put a basket on the neighbor's porch, rang

the doorbell, and ran away.

6. _____   The neighbor answered the door and found the basket, she

was surprised.

7. _____   May Day used to be a very common celebration and an exciting

day. However, not many Americans celebrate May Day today.

Exercise 3

On another piece of paper, combine the following sentences using transition words.

Valentine's Day

1. On Valentine's Day, people in the United States and Canada often give
   cards to their loved ones.
   They may give their sweetheart flowers, candy, or other gifts.

2. Most people think the holiday was named for Saint Valentine.
   The holiday is probably based on a much earlier Roman custom.

3. Much later, in England, birds were thought to choose their mates on Valentine's Day.

   It became known as a day for love.

4. Now elementary schoolchildren often buy or make Valentine's Day cards to exchange with their classmates.

   Many classes have a Valentine's Day party and eat heart-shaped cookies.

5. Girlfriends, boyfriends, husbands, and wives expect to receive some kind of Valentine's card or gift.

   They may feel disappointed or angry.

6. Chocolate is a romantic gift.

   Americans and Canadians buy and give more chocolate around Valentine's Day than any other time of the year.

Writing Practice (Optional)

Write Ten Perfect Compound Sentences with transition words. Use a variety of transition words. You may want to write about a holiday (or holidays) you enjoy or about another topic your teacher suggests. *(See pages 30–32 for instructions and examples.)*

Writing Topics

Your teacher may ask you to write a paragraph or essay on one of the following topics:

1. Describe a holiday from your culture.

   (Description)

2. Compare the celebration of the same holiday in two different places. For example, compare how Near Year's Day is celebrated in China and Canada.

   (Comparison)

3. Create a new holiday. Make up a new holiday, such as Students' Day or Yellow Day. Describe when, how, and why someone should celebrate it.

   (Description / Reasons)

Answer Key to Chapter 3 — More Formal Compound Sentences

Exercise 1

                                S   V   and   S

Americans have a Thanksgiving holiday every fall; in addition, Canadians

 V   S   V

celebrate Thanksgiving in the fall. Canadians celebrate Thanksgiving on the

                                 but   S   (hv) V

second Monday in October; however, in the U.S. Thanksgiving is celebrated

                                                        S

on the fourth Thursday in November. Long ago, the early European settlers

  V   V   so   S   V

survived a hard winter and had successful crops; therefore, they prepared a

big meal together with their Indian neighbors and friends to thank God.

                          S   V

Nowadays, people in both countries get together with their families and

friends to eat a big dinner with traditional foods, such as turkey, potatoes,

                       and   S V

and pumpkin pie; moreover, they use this day to express their thankfulness

                                      S (hv)   V   or

for life. On Thanksgiving Day, we should not eat too much; otherwise,

  S (hv) V

we may feel sick.

Exercise 2

                              S V   S V

1. __C__ May 1st is a holiday in many countries; it is a day for workers.

                              S V

2. __I__   May 1st is a big holiday in Europe; however, in North America,

                              S V

        Labor Day is in September.

                              S   (hv) V   S V

3. __C__ May 1st in the U.S. is called "May Day," and it is a kind of
        celebration for spring.

                                S   V

4. __I__   In the past, children danced around a Maypole on this day;

                              S   V

        moreover, people made flower baskets to bring to their

        neighbors.

Answer Key to Chapter 3   More Formal Compound Sentences

(Concluded)

5. __C__   Usually a child put a May basket on the neighbor's porch, rang
                 the doorbell, and ran away.

6. __I__   The neighbor answered the door and found the basket;
             she was surprised.

7. __C__   May Day used to be a very common celebration and an exciting
             day. However, not many Americans celebrate May Day today.

Exercise 3

Suggested answer:

On Valentine's Day, people in the United States and Canada often give cards to their loved ones; in addition, they may give their sweetheart flowers, candy, or other gifts. Most people think the holiday was named for Saint Valentine; however, the holiday is probably based on a much earlier Roman custom. Much later, in England, birds were thought to choose their mates on Valentine's Day; therefore, it became known as a day for love. Now elementary schoolchildren often buy or make Valentine's Day cards to exchange with their classmates; moreover, many classes have a Valentine's Day party and eat heart-shaped cookies. Girlfriends, boyfriends, husbands, and wives expect to receive some kind of Valentine's card or gift; otherwise, they may feel disappointed or angry. Chocolate is a romantic gift; as a result, Americans and Canadians buy and give more chocolate around Valentine's Day than any other time of the year.

Note: There could be more than one transition word if the meaning makes sense; for example, *in addition, moreover,* and *furthermore* all mean *and.*

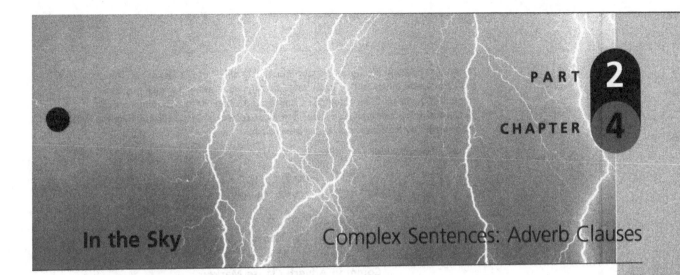

PART **2**

CHAPTER **4**

In the Sky   Complex Sentences: Adverb Clauses

Quick Facts   In the Sky

■ In the most northern areas of North America, including the Yukon Territory, the Northwest Territories, the Arctic Islands, and Alaska, the sun never sets in the summer. This is called the "midnight sun." There are several months of darkness, with no sunshine, in the winter.

■ From 1990 to 1995, there were more than 1,000 tornadoes in North America each year.

■ The rainiest spot in North America is Kauai, Hawaii: 460 inches (1,168 cm) of rain per year.

■ The driest spot in North America is Death Valley, California: 1.63 inches (4.14 cm) of rain per year.

Words to Know

meteorology   The study of weather.

astrology   The study of the positions of the stars, planets, sun, and moon in the belief that they affect human lives.

Leap Year   A year that has an extra day on February 29.

And You?

● What kind of weather is typical in the area (or areas) you have lived?

What is your astrological sign in the Eastern and Western systems? (*See page 56.*)

Do you believe in astrology? Why or why not?

Form

> A complex sentence with an adverb clause has two parts: a simple sentence (independent clause) and a dependent adverb clause (adverb clause marker + subject and verb). It is a complex sentence because it has an independent clause and a dependent clause. The dependent clause is like an adverb because it describes or explains the main clause verb.
>
> These sentences look like this:
>
> S   V   marker + s v
> (SENTENCE   adverb clause)
>
> Marker + s v,   S   V
> (adverb clause,   SENTENCE)
>
> ### Common Adverb Clause Markers
>
> | Cause | Condition | Contrast | Time |
> |-------|-----------|----------|------|
> | because | if | although | after |
> | since | | even though | before |
> | | | though | when |
> | | | while | since |
> | | | | while |
> | | | | the next time |
> | | | | whenever |
>
> *Note:* Adverb clause markers are sometimes called *subordinating conjunctions.*

Example Sentences

Note the adverb clause markers, subjects, and verbs in the following adverb clause sentences about a snowstorm.

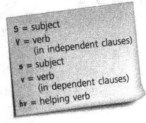

```
     s        v               marker   s    v
```
1. Many students were late for class because it snowed this morning.
   (cause)

```
marker  s   v                         s    hv  hv    v
```
2. If it snows a lot tomorrow, classes may be canceled.
   (condition)

```
     marker        s     v          s     hv    v
```
3. Although the snow was a problem, classes were held as usual.
   (contrast—unexpected result)

```
     s       hv    v                    v
```
4. Students should listen to the radio or watch TV for a school closing report
```
   marker  s    v
```
   when it snows.
   (time)

Note: Use a comma to separate the clauses if the adverb clause comes at the beginning of the sentence. If the adverb clause is second, there is usually no comma.

Watch (Out) For . . .

A In formal written English, the adverb clause cannot stand alone. It is a fragment, which is an incomplete sentence.

No: James was late for class. Because his car got stuck in the snow.

Yes: James was late for class because his car got stuck in the snow.

B Use a compound sentence or an adverb clause complex sentence, but not both!

No: Although the weather was horrible, but classes were held as usual.

Yes: The weather was horrible, but classes were held as usual.

Yes: Although the weather was horrible, classes were held as usual.

Yes: Classes were held as usual although the weather was horrible.

C Use *although, even though,* or *though* to show contrast (unexpected result). Do not use *even* by itself.

No: Even it was snowing, classes were held as usual.

Yes: Even though it was snowing, classes were held as usual.

Yes: Though it was snowing, classes were held as usual.

Yes: Although it was snowing, classes were held as usual.

Notice

1. Several adverb clause markers can have two meanings.

I've loved snow **since** I was a child. (*since* = time)

It can be hard to drive in a snowstorm **since** it's difficult to see. (*since* = reason)

While I was walking to school, I slipped and fell on the ice. (*while* = time)

While winters in Montreal are very snowy, winters in Victoria are usually rainy. (*while* = different or opposite)

2. Some adverb clause markers can also be prepositions (prep).

　　　　　　S hv hv　　　V　　marker s v
Yes: It's been snowing since I got up this morning.
　　　　　(*adverb clause sentence*)

　　　　　　S hv hv　　　V　　prep
Yes: It's been snowing since 3:00.   (*simple sentence*)

　　　　　　S V　　　　　　　　　　　　　　marker s　v
Yes: I plan to put snow tires on my car before I drive to work.
　　　　　(*adverb clause sentence*)

　　　　　　S V　　　　　　　　　　　　　　prep
Yes: I plan to put snow tires on my car before Monday.
　　　　　(*simple sentence*)

Sentence Practice

Exercise 1

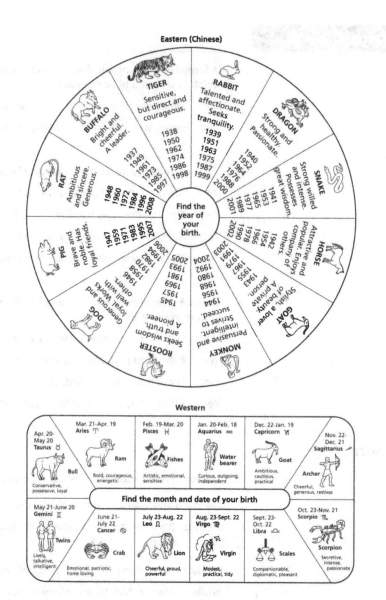

In the following paragraph, underline the adverb clauses and write what kind of clause it is: time, cause, condition, or contrast. Then mark the subjects and verbs in the sentences. The first sentence is done for you.

Astrology, East and West

<u>S   V   S   V</u>

<u>Since people began looking in the sky</u>, they have wondered about the

time

influence of stars. According to astrology, a person's future life depends on

the position of the stars and planets when he or she was born. While the

Western system of astrology is based on twelve "signs" according to the date of birth, the Eastern system of astrology is based on the year of birth. For example, if a girl is born on March 15, 2003, she will be a "Pisces" in Western astrology. When you look at the Eastern system, she will be a "sheep." Many people read their horoscope in the daily newspaper because they believe in astrology. Other people read their horoscope even though they don't believe the predictions. They do it because it is entertaining.

Exercise 2

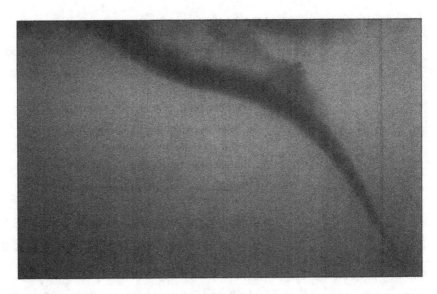

Join sentences together to fix the fragments in the following paragraph. The first one is done for you.

Tornadoes

A tornado (also called a *twister* or *cyclone*) is a dark, narrow, round wind storm. Tornadoes usually occur in the flat middle part of the United States and Canada. When there is a mixture of warm, low wet air and cooler, drier air at high levels, A tornado could form. Tornadoes can have circular winds up to 320 to 480 kilometers (200–300 miles) per hour. Tornadoes can be very dangerous and can destroy buildings and trees. If they touch the ground.

Whenever there is a tornado. You should go to the basement or the cellar in a house or building. You should lie flat on the ground. If you are outside during a tornado. Although there can be many tornadoes in a year. Most of them do not cause any damage.

Exercise 3

On another piece of paper, combine the following groups of sentences using adverb clauses. Use *if, when, because* (two times), *since, though,* and *although*. Think carefully about the meaning and the punctuation.

Leap Year

1. It takes the Earth 365 1/4 days to travel around the sun.
   The modern Western calendar has only 365 days per year.

2. We have Leap Year Day on February 29.
   It helps our calendar fit in the extra time.

3. The year can be divided by the number 4.*
   We add an extra day on February 29.

4. Leap Year occurs only every fourth year.
   People with birthdays or anniversaries on Leap Day have an unusual situation.

5. My friend Sara was born on February 29.
   She celebrates a birthday once every four years.

6. Sara has celebrated only five birthdays.
   She has actually lived for twenty years.

7. People ask Sara about her age.
   She answers, "five or twenty."

* *Note:* We do not add a Leap Day in years that end in 00 (such as 100) if they cannot be divided by 4. There is no Leap Year Day in the year 2100, 2300, or 2500, for example.

Writing Practice (Optional)

Write Ten Perfect Adverb Clause Complex Sentences. Use a variety of adverbs and types of adverb clause sentences (time, reason, condition, contrast). You may want to write about the weather in places you have lived, the traditional calendar in some part of the world, or about another topic your teacher suggests. *(See pages 30–32 for more instructions and examples.)*

Writing Topics

Your teacher may ask you to write a paragraph or essay on one of the following topics.

1. Describe a feature of the climate in a place you have lived. This could include the midnight sun, sandstorms, very cold winters, soft rains, hurricanes, perfect spring days, and so on.

   (Description)

2. Astrology is one way to predict the future. Describe any other ways you know to predict the future or to predict good or bad luck. Do you believe in these?

   (Description / Reasons)

3. Find descriptions of your personality according to Western and / or Eastern astrology. Do the descriptions seem to fit your sense of yourself. Why or why not?

   (Reasons)

Answer Key to Chapter 4 — Complex Sentences: Adverb Clauses

Exercise 1

Since people began looking in the sky, they have wondered about the [time] influence of stars. According to astrology, a person's future life depends on the position of the stars and planets when he or she was born [time]. While the [contrast] Western system of astrology is based on twelve "signs" according to the date of birth, the Eastern or Chinese system of astrology is based on the year of birth. For example, if a girl is born on March 15, 2003 [condition], she will be a "Pisces" in Western astrology. When you look at the Eastern system [time], she will be a "sheep." Many people read their horoscope in the daily newspaper because [cause] they believe in astrology. Other people read their horoscope even though they [contrast] don't believe the predictions. They do it because it is entertaining [cause].

Exercise 2

A tornado (also called a *twister* or *cyclone*) is a dark, narrow, round wind storm. Tornadoes usually occur in the flat middle part of the United States and Canada. When there is a mixture of warm, low wet air and cooler, drier air at high levels, a tornado could form. Tornadoes can have circular winds up to 320 to 480 kilometers (200–300 miles) per hour. Tornadoes can be very dangerous and can destroy buildings and trees if they touch the ground. Whenever there is a tornado, you should go to the basement or the cellar in a house or building. You should lie flat on the ground if you are outside during a tornado. Although there can be many tornadoes in a year, most of them do not cause any damage.

Answer Key to Chapter 4   Complex Sentences: Adverb Clauses

(Concluded)

Exercise 3

<u>Although</u> / <u>Though</u> it takes the Earth 365 1/4 days to travel around the sun, the modern Western calendar has only 365 days per year. We have Leap Year Day on February 29 <u>because</u> / <u>since</u> it helps our calendar fit in the extra time. <u>If</u> / <u>When</u> the year can be divided by the number 4, we add an extra day on February 29. <u>Because</u> / <u>Since</u> Leap Year occurs only every fourth year, people with birthdays or anniversaries on Leap Day have an unusual situation. <u>Since</u> / <u>Because</u> my friend Sara was born on February 29, she celebrates a birthday once every four years. Sara has celebrated only five birthdays <u>though</u> / <u>although</u> she has actually lived for twenty years. <u>When</u> / <u>If</u> people ask Sara about her age, she answers, "five or twenty."

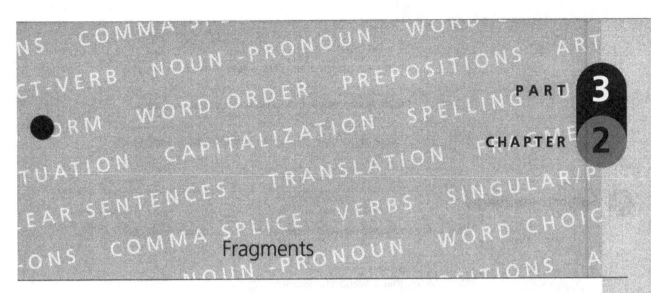

PART **3**

CHAPTER **2**

Fragments

A fragment is an incomplete sentence. Some fragments, such as a sentence with no verb, are ESL errors. Other fragments, such as incomplete sentences that begin with the words *because* or *if* can be used in informal writing, but are not OK in formal writing. Native speakers of English can also have problems with these.

A Subjects

Look at these sentences. What is the difference between the correct and incorrect sentences?

No: I think is a plan that will succeed.

Yes: I think **it** is a plan that will succeed.

No: In my hometown, is a famous statue of my great grandfather.

Yes: In my hometown, **there** is a famous statue of my great grandfather.

- Every sentence and clause needs a subject (unless it is a command).
- Use *there* to introduce a noun that hasn't been mentioned yet.

Exercise 1

Check (✓) the sentences that have no mistakes.

Opinions about UFOs

1. _____   I think are real.

2. _____   In my opinion a fantasy.

3. _____   Is an interesting possibility.

4. _____   I hope are UFOs because life would be more interesting.

5. _____   I think is impossible that people live on other planets.

6. _____   If there are people from other planets, I hope are friendly.

B   Subjects and Verbs

What is the difference between these correct and incorrect sentences?

S = subject
V = verb
hv = helping verb

                                    S
No: My mother a wonderful woman.

                S   V
Yes: My mother **is** a wonderful woman.

                S   s   v
No: A time which I remember best.

                S   s   v   V
Yes: A time which I remember best **was** with a group of friends.

                                    S
No: The man standing in front of the telescope studying the scenery.

                S   hv   V
Yes: The man standing in front of the telescope **is studying** the scenery.

                                    S
No: The papers sent by express mail.

                S   hv   V
Yes: The papers **were sent** by express mail.

                                    S
No: A growing child lots of support.

                S   V
Yes: A growing child **needs** lots of support.

                S
No: Studying for a final exam stressful.

                S   V
Yes: Studying for a final exam **is** stressful.

- Every subject (S) needs a verb (V) to go with it. The verb must be complete.

Exercise 2

Write *C* for correct and *I* for incorrect. Then correct the mistakes and circle *yes* or *no*.

What's Your Opinion?

                                                              Agree or disagree?

1. _____ Learning to write English easy.   yes   no

2. _____ English spelling doesn't make sense.   yes   no

3. _____ Natural English spoken very quickly.   yes   no

4. _____ A British accent the easiest English accent   yes   no
            to understand.

5. _____ English can be learned well in less than   yes   no
            a year.

C Adverb Clauses

These words form dependent adverb clauses: *if, unless, before, after, when, while, since, because, although.* They do not form complete sentences.

Look at these sentences. Can you find the fragments?

No: If my dream comes true.

Yes: If my dream comes true, I will be shocked.

No: When I was a child in my country. I enjoyed playing baseball.

Yes: When I was a child in my country, I enjoyed playing baseball.

No: Because Chinese is the most spoken language in the world.

Yes: Because Chinese is the most spoken language in the world, I'd like to
      learn more about it.

No: I plan to study Chinese. Because it is the most spoken language in
      the world.

Yes: I plan to study Chinese because it is the most spoken language in
      the world.

• Dependent clauses need to be connected to another sentence.

Exercise 3   Check (✓) the sentences that are fragments.

What has been the happiest moment in your life so far?

1. _____   When my first child was born. I was amazed.

2. _____   I think my wedding day was the best time of my life. Because my husband and I were so in love.

3. _____   Although I don't remember it, my birth was probably the best day of my life. Because I am here now.

4. _____   While I was on the bus one day. I met an interesting man and he became my husband of forty years!

5. _____   The day after I graduated from college, I was offered an unbelievable job. I was amazed. Since I was so young.

6. _____   I think it is bad luck if I tell you.

D Reduced Clauses

Sometimes you can reduce clauses as follows:

>   While he was watching the fans cheer, . . .

> *or*   While watching the fans cheer, . . .

> *or*   Watching the fans cheer, . . .

The reduced phrase must be connected to another sentence. It cannot be alone. If it is alone, it is a fragment.

No: Watching the fans cheer.

Yes: Watching the fans cheer, the man felt the excitement of the crowd.

E Prepositional Phrases, Infinitives, and Gerunds

Prepositional phrases, infinitives, and gerunds are fragments if they are alone in a sentence.

No: In the middle of the summer during a tense afternoon.

Yes: In the middle of the summer during a tense afternoon, I remembered the discussion we had.

No: To write an interesting journal for the teacher to read.

Yes: To write an interesting journal for the teacher to read, try writing about a personal experience.

No: Swimming ten laps in a cool pool in the early morning.

Yes: Swimming ten laps in a cool pool in the early morning is her favorite kind of exercise.

Exercise 4

Check (✓) the sentences that are fragments.

My Conversational Strengths

1. _____ Speaking to other people.

2. _____ In conversation with quiet people, I encourage them to talk more.

3. _____ When talking to my friends. I joke a lot.

4. _____ Helping people feel comfortable, especially shy people, is a strength I have.

5. _____ While listening carefully to other people.

6. _____ When participating in a conversation, I pay attention to what people say.

7. _____ To not interrupt other people when they are talking.

8. _____ With a large group of people who like to talk a lot.

F *Especially, Such As, For Example*

Look at these sentences. What is the difference between the correct and incorrect sentences?

No: She needs to study more. Especially grammar and vocabulary.

Yes: She needs to study more, especially grammar and vocabulary.

No: To improve your listening, I recommend practice. Such as listening to tapes and talking to native speakers.

Yes: To improve your listening, I recommend activities such as listening to tapes and talking to native speakers.

No: There are several causes of heart disease. For example, smoking and cholesterol.

Yes: There are several causes of heart disease, for example, smoking and cholesterol.

- *Especially, such as,* and *for example* cannot begin sentences unless they are followed by a subject and a verb (an independent clause).

Exercise 5

Correct the mistakes.

What was the most helpful advice your parents or grandparents gave you?

1. They taught me to be kind to others. Especially the poor, the sick and the elderly.

2. It is important to treat everyone well. For example, with respect and honesty.

3. My grandparents never allowed me to do dishonest things. Such as lie to them.

4. They gave me a lot of advice. For example, to be patient with others, try to understand their situation, and not judge them.

5. They always encouraged me to work hard. Especially when I didn't think I could be successful.

G Connecting Main Verbs

No: He came late, didn't study, got many absences.
No: He came late, and didn't study, and got many absences.
Yes: He came late, didn't study, and got many absences.

No: He's studying, working two jobs, taking care of his family.
Yes: He's studying, working two jobs, and taking care of his family.

- With three or more main verbs, use a connecting word (*and, or, but, so*) before the main verb.
- It is not necessary to repeat the same subject or *be* verb.

Exercise 6

Correct the mistakes.

What do you think about fast food restaurants?

1. There are too many and the food is unhealthy and they are expensive.

2. I love to eat hamburgers, drink milk shakes, not worry about calories.

3. I am used to buying fresh foods, cooking them myself, not eating

   fattening foods.

4. For me they are very convenient, cheap, fast.

5. I like them and go often, I don't think they are very healthy.

Chapter Review

Exercise 7

Check (✓) the sentences that are fragments. Then correct the mistakes.

Being Single vs. Being Married

What are some advantages to being single?

1. _____ You can do what you want. When you want.

2. _____ If you don't feel like cooking, you don't have to.

3. _____ Going out and meeting new people. It's easy.

4. _____ People who are single more freedom.

5. _____ When you are single. You can spend your money any way

   you want.

What are some advantages to being married?

6. _____ There always someone to do things with.

7. _____ I think that having a partner and not feeling lonely.

8. _____ If you have someone to help you, life is easier.

9. _____ I can think of two advantages. For example, having someone

   to care about and having someone to take care of you.

10. _____ The other person can cook. When you are tired.

Exercise 8

Write C for correct and I for incorrect. Then correct the mistakes.

Advice from Teenagers to Parents

1. _____   When you are angry and want to talk to your child. Wait until you calm down.

2. _____   Understanding how your teenager feels when he or she is upset.

3. _____   You don't have to be so serious just because you are the parent.

4. _____   I think it important to have patience.

5. _____   Try to remember how you felt when you a teenager.

6. _____   To have a close relationship with your kids, listen carefully.

7. _____   Teenagers wanting more freedom.

8. _____   The best advice is spending time with your children, listening

to them, trying to understand the way they are feeling.

Exercise 9

Correct the mistakes.

Kinds of Movies I Like

My favorite kinds of movies are romance. Such as *Ghost* and *Pretty Woman*. When I was a teenager and chose books. I always wanted to read love stories, imagine a happy ending, dream about a life like that. I like it best. If the story has a happy ending. Other movies that I like mysteries. It exciting to try to figure out the ending. I also like action movies. If they are not too violent. I don't like a lot of guns and bombs. In this country are too many violent movies. One time sitting with my friends and watching an action movie. I covered my eyes because it was too violent. I think I missed most of the movie.

Answer Key to Chapter 2   Fragments

Exercise 1

All of the sentences have mistakes.

Exercise 2

1. __I__ Learning to write English is easy.
2. __C__ English spelling doesn't make sense.
3. __I__ Natural English is spoken very quickly.
4. __I__ A British accent is the easiest English accent to understand.
5. __C__ English can be learned well in less than a year.

Exercise 3

1. ✓ When my first child was born. I was amazed.
2. ✓ I think my wedding day was the best time of my life. Because my husband and I were so in love.
3. ✓ Although I don't remember it, my birth was probably the best day of my life. Because I am here now.
4. ✓ While I was on the bus one day. I met an interesting man and he became my husband of forty years!
5. ✓ The day after I graduated from college, I was offered an unbelievable job. I was amazed. Since I was so young.
6. ____ I think it is bad luck if I tell you.

Exercise 4

1. ✓ Speaking to other people.
2. ____ In conversation with quiet people, I encourage them to talk more.
3. ✓ When talking to my friends. I joke a lot.
4. ____ Helping people feel comfortable, especially shy people, is a strength I have.
5. ✓ While listening carefully to other people.
6. ____ When participating in a conversation, I pay attention to what people say.
7. ✓ To not interrupt other people when they are talking.
8. ✓ With a large group of people who like to talk a lot.

Answer Key to Chapter 2   Fragments

(Continued)

Exercise 5

1. They taught me to be kind to others, <u>especially</u> the poor, the sick and the elderly.

2. It is important to treat everyone well, <u>for</u> example with respect and honesty.

3. My grandparents never allowed me to do dishonest things, <u>such</u> as lie to them.

4. They gave me a lot of advice, <u>for</u> example, to be patient with others, try to understand their situation, and not judge them.

5. They always encouraged me to work hard, <u>especially</u> when I didn't think I could be successful.

Exercise 6

1. There are too many, the food is unhealthy, and they are expensive.

2. I love to eat hamburgers, drink milk shakes, <u>and</u> not worry about calories.

3. I am used to buying fresh foods, cooking them myself, <u>and</u> not eating fattening foods.

4. For me they are very convenient, cheap, <u>and</u> fast.

5. I like them and go often, <u>but</u> I don't think they are very healthy.

Exercise 7

1.   ✓   You can do what you want <u>when</u> you want.

2.   If you don't feel like cooking, you don't have to.

3.   ✓   Going out and meeting new people <u>is</u> easy.

4.   ✓   People who are single <u>have</u> more freedom.

5.   ✓   When you are single, <u>you</u> can spend your money any way you want.

6.   ✓   There <u>is</u> always someone to do things with.

7.   ✓   I think that having a partner and not feeling lonely <u>is</u> . . . (an advantage).

8.   If you have someone to help you, life is easier.

9.   ✓   I can think of two advantages, <u>for</u> example, having someone to care about and having someone to take care of you.

10.   ✓   The other person can cook <u>when</u> you are tired.

Answer Key to Chapter 2   Fragments

(Concluded)

Exercise 8

1. ___I___   When you are angry and want to talk to your child, <u>wait</u> until you calm down.

2. ___I___   Understanding how your teenager feels when he or she is upset <u>is</u> . . . (important).

3. ___C___   You don't have to be so serious just because you are the parent.

4. ___I___   I think it <u>is</u> important to have patience.

5. ___I___   Try to remember how you felt when you <u>were</u> a teenager.

6. ___C___   To have a close relationship with your kids, listen carefully.

7. ___I___   Teenagers <u>want</u> more freedom.

8. ___I___   The best advice is spending time with your children, listening to them, <u>and</u> trying to understand the way they are feeling.

Exercise 9

    My favorite kinds of movies are romance, <u>such</u> as *Ghost* and *Pretty Woman*. When I was a teenager and chose books, I always wanted to read love stories, imagine a happy ending, <u>and</u> dream about a life like that. I like it <u>best if</u> the story has a happy ending. Other movies that I like <u>are</u> mysteries. It <u>is</u> exciting to try to figure out the ending. I also like action <u>movies if</u> they are not too violent. I don't like a lot of guns and bombs. In this country <u>there</u> are too many violent movies. One time sitting with my friends and watching an action movie, I covered my eyes because it was too violent. I think I missed most of the movie.

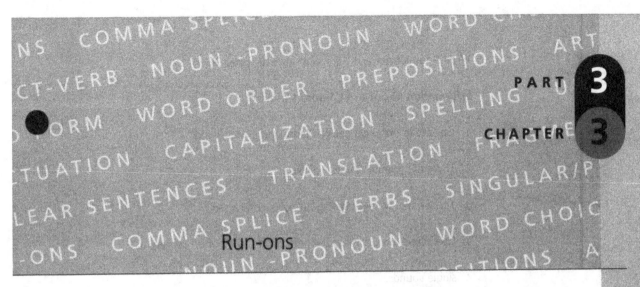

Run-ons

A run-on sentence is a sentence that contains more than one sentence, but it is written as only one sentence. Many times the sentence is too long and should be divided into two or more shorter sentences. Native speakers of English also study this problem.

A Run-on Sentences

What is the difference between the correct and incorrect sentences?

No: The runner went faster the crowd cheered.
(S V   S V)

Yes: The runner went faster. The crowd cheered.
(S V   S V)

No: The movie was very sad many people in the audience cried.
(S V   S   V)

Yes: The movie was very sad. Many people in the audience cried.
(S V   S   V)

No: At first, I felt lonely then, I met some people.
(S V   S V)

Yes: At first, I felt lonely. Then, I met some people.
(S V   S V)

- A complete sentence has a subject and a verb. Run-on sentences are two complete sentences that are written as one sentence.

- One way to correct a run-on sentence is to put a period between the two complete sentences.

Exercise 1

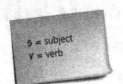

S = subject
V = verb

Write S for subject and V for verb in each sentence.

Information about the Chinese Language

1. Chinese is the most spoken language in the world.

2. There are several Chinese dialects.

3. The writing system uses about 4,000 characters.

4. Characters are usually not single words. They often represent

   single sounds.

5. The tone of a word sometimes changes to give a different meaning.

6. Mandarin Chinese, for example, has four different tones.

Exercise 2

Check (✓) the sentences that are run-ons. (Remember, a run-on occurs when you have S V S V with no punctuation between them.) Then correct the sentences.

Reasons for Studying English

1. _____ It's an international language much of the business world

   speaks it.

2. _____ You can communicate with people from other cultures

   and countries.

3. _____ Learning another language helps you understand other ways

   of thinking.

4. _____ I want to study at a university in an English-speaking country

   my major is computer science.

5. _____ It's interesting it's fun.

B Correcting Run-on Sentences

There are other ways to correct run-on sentences:

1. Use a connecting word *(but, yet, and, so, or)* and a comma before it.

   No: I worked hard I didn't pass.

   Yes: I worked hard, **but** I didn't pass.   (contrast)

   Yes: I worked hard, **yet** I didn't pass.   (contrast)

   Yes: I worked hard, **and** I passed.   (addition)

   Yes: I worked hard, **so** I passed.   (result)

   Yes: I can work hard, **or** I can fail.   (choice)

2. Put a semicolon between the two sentences. A semicolon shows that the two sentences are closely related. A comma is not possible because it cannot be used between two sentences.

   No: The athletes trained for months they were in excellent condition.

   Yes: The athletes trained for months; they were in excellent condition.

3. Make one part of the sentence a dependent clause with words like *because, if, when, before, after*.

   No: He wanted his children to feel special each one got time alone with him.

   Yes: **Because** he wanted his children to feel special, each one got time alone with him.

Exercise 3

Correct the following run-ons using the word or punctuation in parentheses.

Did You Know?

1. The best time to buy shoes is at the end of the day your feet

   are bigger. (because)

2. Shaking a young child is dangerous it can cause brain damage.   (;)

3. Wear pants when you fly on airplanes they will protect your legs if there

   is an accident.   (;)

4. Seahorses are different from other animals the males have

   the babies. (because)

5. Only female bees are worker bees they are the ones that sting.   (, and)

6. Everyone dreams every night some people don't remember

   their dreams.   (, but)

7. The cougar, mountain lion, and puma are the same animal they have

   different names in different places.   (, but)

8. It takes one month for the moon to go around the earth it takes 365 days

   for the earth to go around the sun.   (;)

Chapter Review

Exercise 4

Write C for correct and I for incorrect. Then correct the mistakes.

Internet History

1. _____ The Internet began in 1969 it was an experiment by

   the U.S. government.

2. _____ Originally, the Internet was planned so that academic and military

   people could communicate.

3. _____ At the time, because the government was afraid of nuclear

   attack, it wanted a system that would work during an attack.

4. _____ The government planned it without a main office that someone

   could bomb.

5. _____ Since no one was in charge, it grew in many directions without

   rules or limits.

6. _____ As a result, millions of users are now connected around

   the world.

Exercise 5

Correct the run-ons.

My First Day in This Country

I arrived at 5:30 in the morning I was incredibly tired. My plane ride was 15 hours, and I didn't sleep at all during the flight. When I arrived, there was no one to meet me. My host family had car trouble they were about 15 minutes late. I was very scared I cried a little and wondered why I left my country. Soon my host mother saw me and gave me a big smile she was so kind. I felt better after I met her and her husband. They took me out to breakfast. The food was a little strange, and I didn't speak much English. But they were patient, and we communicated basic information. They wanted to show me a little of the city however I was so tired I asked them if I could sleep first. They took me to their house. I went to bed I slept for 17 hours!

Answer Key to Chapter 3   **Run-ons**

Exercise 1

        S   V
1. Chinese is the most spoken language in the world.

        S   V
2. There are several Chinese dialects.

          S   V
3. The writing system uses about 4,000 characters.

        S   V   S   V
4. Characters are usually not single words. They often represent single sounds.

          S   V
5. The tone of a word sometimes changes to give a different meaning.

        S   V
6. Mandarin Chinese, for example, has four different tones.

Exercise 2

1. ✓ It's an international language. Much of the business world speaks it.

2. ____ You can communicate with people from other cultures and countries.

3. ____ Learning another language helps you understand other ways of thinking.

4. ✓ I want to study at a university in an English-speaking country. My major is computer science.

5. ✓ It's interesting. It's fun.

Exercise 3

1. The best time to buy shoes is at the end of the day because your feet are bigger.

2. Shaking a young child is dangerous; it can cause brain damage.

3. Wear pants when you fly on airplanes; they will protect your legs if there is an accident.

4. Seahorses are different from other animals because the males have the babies.

5. Only female bees are worker bees, and they are the ones that sting.

6. Everyone dreams every night, but some people don't remember their dreams.

7. The cougar, mountain lion, and puma are the same animal, but they have different names in different places.

8. It takes one month for the moon to go around the earth; it takes 365 days for the earth to go around the sun.

Answer Key to Chapter 3   Run-ons

(Concluded)

Exercise 4

1. __I__   The Internet began in 1969. <u>It</u> was an experiment by the U.S. government.

or:

The Internet began in 1969; <u>it</u> was an experiment by the U.S. government.

2. __C__   Originally, the Internet was planned so that academic and military people could communicate.

3. __C__   At the time, because the government was afraid of nuclear attack, it wanted a system that would work during an attack.

4. __C__   The government planned it without a main office that someone could bomb.

5. __C__   Since no one was in charge, it grew in many directions without rules or limits.

6. __C__   As a result, millions of users are now connected around the world.

Exercise 5

I arrived at 5:30 in the morning. I was incredibly tired. My plane ride was 15 hours, and I didn't sleep at all during the flight. When I arrived, there was no one to meet me. My host family had car trouble. <u>They</u> were about 15 minutes late. I was very scared. I cried a little and wondered why I left my country. Soon my host mother saw me and gave me a big smile. <u>She</u> was so kind. I felt better after I met her and her husband. They took me out to breakfast. The food was a little strange, and I didn't speak much English. But they were patient, and we communicated basic information. They wanted to show me a little of the city; <u>however,</u> I was so tired I asked them if I could sleep first. They took me to their house. I went to bed. I slept for 17 hours!

Note: Connecting words can be used instead of periods: I went to bed <u>and</u> slept for 17 hours!

PART **3**

CHAPTER **4**

Comma Splice

A comma splice is a type of run-on sentence. It contains two sentences connected by only a comma, but a comma is not strong enough to separate the two sentences. Native speakers of English also need to edit their writing to avoid comma splices.

A Basic Comma Splice

Can you discover the difference between the correct and incorrect sentences?

*hv = helping verb

No: We'll work together, we'll help each other, we'll succeed.
       S hv* V   S hv V   S hv V

Yes: We'll work together. We'll help each other. We'll succeed.

No: I tried my best, there is nothing more I can do.
       S V   S V

Yes: I tried my best. There is nothing more I can do.

No: I studied really hard, I passed.
       S V   S V

Yes: I studied really hard. I passed.

• Two complete sentences cannot be separated by a comma. A complete sentence has a subject and a verb.

Exercise 1

Find the subject(s) and the verb(s) in each sentence. Write **S** for subject and **V** for verb.

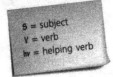

Reggae Music

1. Reggae music comes from Jamaica.

2. It began in the 1960s.

3. The rhythm is slow and the beat is lively.

4. Bob Marley is probably the most famous reggae musician.

5. When he died, classic reggae also died.

Exercise 2

Write **C** for correct and **I** for incorrect. Correct the mistakes. Then mark if the sentence is true or false.

Animal Trivia: True or False?

True or false?

1. _____ Adult horses stand up when they sleep,

   they lie down when they are sick. _____

2. _____ Alligators are supposed to be friendlier

   than crocodiles, they are still dangerous. _____

3. _____ Butterflies can't fly in the mornings.

   Their wings are too heavy with dew. _____

4. _____ People can be identified by their fingerprints,

   dogs can be identified by their nose prints. _____

5. _____ An eagle's nest is very large. It can weigh

   over 500 kilograms. _____

6. _____ Female mosquitoes bite, male mosquitoes don't. _____

B Using Connecting Words

If you use a comma to separate two complete sentences, you also need one of the connecting words: *and, but, yet, so, or, for.*

No: We'll work together, we'll help each other.

Yes: We'll work together, **and** we'll help each other.   (and = addition)

Yes: We'll work together, **but** we may not succeed.   (but = contrast)

Yes: We'll work together, **yet** we may not succeed.   (yet = contrast)

Yes: We'll work together, **so** we can succeed.   (so = result)

Yes: We can work together, **or** we can fail.   (or = choice)

Yes: We'll work together, **for** we want to succeed.   (for = reason / because)

See Run-ons page 105 for other ways of correcting comma splices.

Exercise 3

Correct the sentences using one of the following: *and, but, yet, so, or, for.*

Do you think memorizing school material is a good way to learn?

1. It's useful, you might forget some things.

2. I have a good memory, it's a good method for me.

3. It's good for vocabulary, there are so many words.

4. It's not fun, it's important.

5. I wasn't a good student, I don't remember ever memorizing anything.

6. In school I had to memorize a lot of poetry. I still remember it,

   I guess it's useful.

7. I memorize speeches, I will forget them.

8. Some things you need to memorize, some things you can only

   learn by doing.

9. Important facts can be memorized, ideas should be discussed.

10. I memorize things that don't have many rules, like gerunds

    and infinitives, I will go crazy.

Chapter Review

Exercise 4

Correct the mistakes.

How have computers affected your life?

1. I used to send my family a lot of faxes, now I use e-mail because

    it's cheaper.

2. Actually, I don't know how to use them, I need to take some classes.

3. I only do word processing, it really helps me do my school work faster.

4. I love the Internet, instead of watching TV or playing video games,

    I spend a lot of time surfing the Internet.

5. Computers still seem complicated to me, I'm a little afraid of them.

6. I love the Spell Check, I save so much time because I don't need to always

    look in my dictionary when I write a paper.

Exercise 5

Correct the mistakes by putting periods (.) where necessary.

The Perfect Job for Me

There are several jobs I'm interested in, all of them allow me to work with

my hands. I love to build things by hand. Sometimes I think about furniture

making, I'm talking about regular furniture, I mean furniture made with

beautiful woods, like cherry or oak. But that is probably a hard way to earn

money to support a family. I am also interested in repairing antique cars, I

love working with the engines and also making the outside of the car look

beautiful again. Whatever job I choose, there is one thing that is very

important to me. I don't want to work from 8:00 to 5:00, I want to decide

my own hours. Maybe I will begin working at 11 A.M. and finish at midnight.

Or I can wake up early with the birds and work until midday. My job needs to

have a flexible schedule.

Answer Key to Chapter 4   Comma Splice

Exercise 1

1. Reggae music comes from Jamaica.
   $\overset{S}{}\quad\overset{V}{}$

2. It began in the 1960s.
   $\overset{S}{}\ \overset{V}{}$

3. The rhythm is slow, and the beat is lively.
   $\overset{S}{}\quad\overset{V}{}\qquad\overset{S}{}\quad\overset{V}{}$

4. Bob Marley is probably the most famous reggae musician.
   $\overset{S}{}\quad\overset{V}{}$

5. When he died, classic reggae also died.
   $\overset{S}{}\ \overset{V}{}\qquad\overset{S}{}\quad\overset{V}{}$

Exercise 2

1. __I__   Adult horses stand up when they sleep. They lie down when they are sick.   (T)

2. __I__   Alligators are supposed to be friendlier than crocodiles. They are still dangerous.   (T)

3. __C__   Butterflies can't fly in the mornings. Their wings are too heavy with dew.   (T)

4. __I__   People can be identified by their fingerprints. Dogs can be identified by their nose prints.   (T)

5. __C__   An eagle's nest is very large. It can weigh over 500 kilograms.   (T)

6. __I__   Female mosquitoes bite. Male mosquitoes don't.   (T)

Exercise 3

1. It's useful, but / yet you might forget some things.

2. I have a good memory, so it's a good method for me.

3. It's good for vocabulary, but / yet / for there are so many words.

4. It's not fun, but / yet it's important.

5. I wasn't a good student, so / and I don't remember ever memorizing anything.

6. In school I had to memorize a lot of poetry. I still remember it, so I guess it's useful.

7. I memorize speeches, or / but / yet / for I will forget them.

8. Some things you need to memorize, and / but / yet some things you can only learn by doing.

9. Important facts can be memorized, but / yet ideas should be discussed.

10. I memorize things that don't have many rules, like gerunds and infinitives, or I will go crazy.

Answer Key to Chapter 4   Comma Splice

(Concluded)

Exercise 4

1. I used to send my family a lot of faxes. <u>Now</u> I use e-mail because it's cheaper.

2. Actually, I don't know how to use them. <u>I</u> need to take some classes.

3. I only do word processing. <u>It</u> really helps me do my school work faster.

4. I love the Internet. <u>Instead</u> of watching TV or playing video games, I spend a lot of time surfing the Internet.

5. Computers still seem complicated to me. <u>I'm</u> a little afraid of them.

6. I love the Spell Check. <u>I</u> save so much time because I don't need to always look in my dictionary when I write a paper.

Note: Comma + connecting word can be used. A semicolon can also be used.

Exercise 5

There are several jobs I'm interested in. <u>All</u> of them allow me to work with my hands. I love to build things by hand. Sometimes I think about furniture making. <u>I'm</u> talking about regular furniture. <u>I</u> mean furniture made with beautiful woods, like cherry or oak. But that is probably a hard way to earn money to support a family. I am also interested in repairing antique cars. <u>I</u> love working with the engines and also making the outside of the car look beautiful again. Whatever job I choose, there is one thing that is very important to me. I don't want to work from 8:00 to 5:00. <u>I</u> want to decide my own hours. Maybe I will begin working at 11 A.M. and finish at midnight. Or I can wake up early with the birds and work until midday. My job needs to have a flexible schedule.

Note: Comma + connecting word can also be used. A semicolon can also be used.

CHAPTER

23

Capital Letters

INTRODUCTORY ACTIVITY

You probably know a good deal about the uses of capital letters. Answering the questions below will help you check your knowledge.

1. Write the full name of a person you know: _____

2. In what city and state were you born? _____

3. What is your present street address? _____

4. Name a country where you would like to travel: _____

5. Name a school that you attended: _____

6. Give the name of a store where you buy food: _____

7. Name a company where you or anyone you know

   works: _____

8. Which day of the week is the busiest for you? _____

9. What holiday is your favorite? _____

10. Which brand of toothpaste do you use? _____

11. Give the brand name of a candy you like: _____

12. Name a song or a television show you enjoy: _____

13. Write the title of a magazine or newspaper you

    read: _____

Items 14–16

Three capital letters are needed in the example below. Underline the words you think should be capitalized. Then write them, capitalized, in the spaces provided.

> on Super Bowl Sunday, my roommate said, "let's buy some snacks and invite a few friends over to watch the game." i knew my plans to write a term paper would have to be changed.

14. _____   15. _____   16. _____

Main Uses of Capital Letters

Capital letters are used with:

1. First word in a sentence or direct quotation
2. Names of persons and the word *I*
3. Names of particular places
4. Names of days of the week, months, and holidays
5. Names of commercial products
6. Titles of books, magazines, articles, films, television shows, songs, poems, stories, papers that you write, and the like
7. Names of companies, associations, unions, clubs, religious and political groups, and other organizations

Each use is illustrated on the pages that follow.

First Word in a Sentence or Direct Quotation

Our company has begun laying people off.

The doctor said, "This may hurt a bit."

"My husband," said Martha, "is a light eater. When it's light, he starts to eat."

EXPLANATION: In the third example above, *My* and *When* are capitalized because they start new sentences. But *is* is not capitalized because it is part of the first sentence.

Names and Titles

Names of Persons and the Word I

At the picnic, I met Tony Curry and Lola Morrison.

Names of Particular Places

After graduating from Gibbs High School in Houston, I worked for a summer at a nearby Holiday Inn on Clairmont Boulevard.

But   Use small letters if the specific name of a place is not given.

After graduating from high school in my hometown, I worked for a summer at a nearby hotel on one of the main shopping streets.

Names of Days of the Week, Months, and Holidays

This year, Memorial Day falls on the last Thursday in May.

But   Use small letters for the seasons—summer, fall, winter, and spring.

In the early summer and fall, my hay fever bothers me.

Names of Commercial Products

The consumer magazine gave high ratings to Cheerios breakfast cereal, Breyer's ice cream, and Progresso chicken noodle soup.

But   Use small letters for the *type* of product (breakfast cereal, ice cream, chicken noodle soup, and the like).

Titles of Books, Magazines, Articles, Films, Television Shows, Songs, Poems, Stories, Papers That You Write, and the Like

My oral report was on *The Diary of a Young Girl*, by Anne Frank.

While watching *All My Children* on television, I thumbed through *Cosmopolitan* magazine and the *New York Times*.

Names of Companies, Associations, Unions, Clubs, Religious and Political Groups, and Other Organizations

A new bill before Congress is opposed by the National Rifle Association.

My wife is Jewish; I am Roman Catholic. We are both members of the Democratic Party.

My parents have life insurance with Prudential, auto insurance with Allstate, and medical insurance with United Healthcare.

Capitalizing Names and Titles	ACTIVITY 1

In the sentences that follow, cross out the words that need capitals. Then write the capitalized forms of the words in the space provided. The number of spaces tells you how many corrections to make in each case.

EXAMPLE

Rhoda said, "~~why~~ should I bother to *eat* this ~~hershey~~ bar? I should just apply it directly to my hips." ___Why___ ___Hershey___

> HINT   The word *I* and names of organizations are capitalized.

1. Sometimes i still regret not joining the boy scouts when I was in grade school.

   _____ _____ _____

2. On the friday after thanksgiving, Carole went to target to buy gifts for her family.

   _____ _____ _____

328   PART 3   Sentence Skills

3. In the box office of the regal cinema is a sign saying, "if you plan to see an R-rated movie, be ready to show your ID."

    _____   _____   _____   _____

4. In many new england towns, republicans are substantially outnumbered by democrats.

    _____   _____   _____   _____

5. Nelson was surprised to learn that both state farm and nationwide have insurance offices in the prudential building.

    _____   _____   _____   _____

6. Magazines such as *time* and *newsweek* featured articles about the fires that devastated part of southern california.

    _____   _____   _____   _____

7. The rose grower whom Steve works for said that the biggest rose-selling holidays are valentine's day and mother's day.

    _____   _____   _____   _____

8. With some pepsis and fritos nearby, the kids settled down to play a game on the macintosh computer.

    _____   _____   _____   _____

9. Bob's ford taurus was badly damaged when he struck a deer last saturday.

    _____   _____   _____   _____

10. Though Julie Andrews excelled in the broadway version of *my fair lady,* Audrey Hepburn was cast as the female lead in the movie version.

    _____   _____   _____   _____

Other Uses of Capital Letters

Capital letters are also used with:

- Names that show family relationships
- Titles of persons when used with their names
- Specific school courses
- Languages
- Geographic locations
- Historic periods and events
- Races, nations, and nationalities
- Opening and closing of a letter

Each use is illustrated on the pages that follow.

Names and Titles

Names That Show Family Relationships

Aunt Sally and Uncle Jack are selling their house.

I asked Grandfather to start the fire.

Is Mother feeling better?

But   Do not capitalize words such as *mother, father, grandmother, grandfather, uncle, aunt,* and so on when they are preceded by *my* or another possessive word.

My aunt and uncle are selling their house.

I asked my grandfather to start the fire.

Is my mother feeling better?

Titles of Persons When Used with Their Names

I wrote an angry letter to Senator Blutt.

Can you drive to Dr. Stein's office?

We asked Professor Bushkin about his attendance policy.

But   Use small letters when titles appear by themselves, without specific names.

I wrote an angry letter to my senator.

Can you drive to the doctor's office?

We asked our professor about his attendance policy.

Specific School Courses

My courses this semester include Accounting I, Introduction to Computer Science, Business Law, General Psychology, and Basic Math.

But   Use small letters for general subject areas.

This semester I'm taking mostly business courses, but I have a psychology course and a math course as well.

Miscellaneous Categories

Languages

Lydia speaks English and Spanish equally well.

Geographic Locations

I lived in the South for many years and then moved to the West Coast.

But   Use small letters in giving directions.

Go south for about five miles and then bear west.

Historic Periods and Events

One essay question dealt with the Battle of the Bulge in World War II.

330   PART 3   Sentence Skills

Races, Nations, and Nationalities

> The census form asked whether I was African American, Native American, Hispanic, or Asian.
>
> Last summer I hitchhiked through Italy, France, and Germany.
>
> The city is a melting pot for Koreans, Vietnamese, and Mexican Americans.

But   Use small letters when referring to *whites* or *blacks*.

> Both whites and blacks supported our mayor in the election.

Opening and Closing of a Letter

Dear Sir:	Sincerely yours,
Dear Madam:	Truly yours,

Capitalize only the first word in a closing.

ACTIVITY 2   **Where Is Capitalization Needed?**

Cross out the words that need capitals in the following sentences. Then write the capitalized forms of the words in the spaces provided. The number of spaces tells you how many corrections to make in each case.

1. My uncle david, who has cirrhosis of the liver, added his name to the national waiting list for organ transplants.

   _____   _____

2. My daughter asked me to buy her a magenta pink motorola razr phone and bluetooth headset for her sixteenth birthday.

   _____   _____

3. Former united states president jimmy carter received the nobel peace prize in 2002.

   _____   _____   _____   _____   _____

   _____   _____   _____

4. Terisa spoke to the class about her experience as a pacific islander from samoa who is now living on the east coast.

   _____   _____   _____   _____

   _____

5. Next semester, I want to register for principles of marketing and two other business courses.

   _____   _____

Unnecessary Use of Capitals

| **Where Is Capitalization Unnecessary?** | **ACTIVITY 3** |

Many errors in capitalization are caused by adding capitals where they are not needed. Cross out the incorrectly capitalized letters in the following sentences and write the correct forms in the spaces provided. The number of spaces tells you how many corrections to make in each sentence.

1. Everyone waits for Mariko's Husband, who is from Texas, to make his famous Barbeque Ribs.

   _____ _____ _____

2. One of Stuart's English professors at his Community College worked for Google as a Technical Writer.

   _____ _____ _____ _____

3. The Electronics Store at Meadowland Mall is having a sale on Televisions and DVD Players.

   _____ _____ _____ _____

4. Several Community Organizations are sponsoring a Food Drive at the neighborhood homeless shelter.

   _____ _____ _____ _____

5. Bridget spoke to her daughter's Science Teacher about the upcoming field trip to the Tidal Pools at Sunset Grove Beach.

   _____ _____ _____ _____

| **Editing and Rewriting** | **ACTIVITY 4** |

Working with a partner, read the short paragraph below and mark off the fifteen spots where capital letters are missing. Then use the space provided to rewrite the passage, adding capital letters where needed. Feel free to discuss the passage quietly with your partner and refer back to the chapter when necessary.

Personal

[1]The morning that I visited the lincoln memorial, it was raining. [2]It was a quiet thursday in late october, and the air was cold. [3]I was with uncle walt, and we had spent the morning visiting the smithsonian institution together. [4]After lunch, my uncle said to me, "now we're going to go someplace that you'll never forget." [5]When we arrived, I was overwhelmed by lincoln's massive statue, which dwarfed everything around it—just as the man had done in life. [6]To my left I was aware of the

continued

silently flowing potomac river. [7]Engraved on one of the marble walls was the gettysburg address. [8]I read those familiar words and remained there for a time in silence, touched by the simple eloquence of that speech. [9]I then snapped just one picture with my kodak camera and walked down the stone steps quietly. [10]The photograph still sits on my desk today as a reminder of that special visit.

_____

_____

_____

_____

_____

_____

_____

_____

_____

_____

ACTIVITY 5   Creating Sentences

Working with a partner, write a sentence (or two) as directed. Pay special attention to capital letters.

1. Write about a place you like (or want) to visit. Be sure to give the name of the place, including the city, state, or country where it is located.

2. Write a sentence (or two) in which you state the name of your elementary school, your favorite teacher or subject, and your least favorite teacher or subject.

3. Write a sentence (or two) that includes the names of three brand-name products that you often use. You may begin the sentence with the words, "Three brand-name products I use every day are . . ."

4. Think of the name of your favorite musical artist or performer. Then write a sentence in which you include the musician's name and the title of one of his or her songs.

5. Write a sentence in which you describe something you plan to do two days from now. Be sure to include the date and day of the week.

REFLECTIVE ACTIVITY

1. What would writing be like without capital letters? Use an example or two to help show how capital letters are important to writing.

2. What three uses of capital letters are most difficult for you to remember? Explain, giving examples.

REVIEW TEST 1

Cross out the words that need capitals in the following sentences. Then write the capitalized forms of the words in the spaces provided. The number of spaces tells you how many corrections to make for each item.

EXAMPLE

At the ~~society~~ of ~~american~~ ~~travel writers~~ conference this year, I had the pleasure of listening to ~~sarah jones~~, a travel agent with more than forty years of experience.

____Society____   ____American____   ____Travel Writers____   ____Sarah Jones____

1. "Traveling is my favorite pastime," explained ms. jones. "over the years i've learned that the location of the hotel can really make a difference in a vacation."

_____   _____   _____   _____

2. She told the audience that in places like new york city and chicago, location is very important.

_____   _____

3. Visitors usually want to be close to the sites, so staying in a suburb like yonkers or schaumburg could add hours of drive time to get to the site.

_____   _____

4. Ms. Jones then gave advice about international travel. She told the audience that in a city like rome, italy, visitors who are interested in seeing the vatican might want to consider the sant'Anna hotel, as it is located just a short walk away.

_____   _____   _____   _____   _____

5. However, if spending time in the roman forum is the visitor's priority, then the kolbe hotel rome would be a better choice.

_____   _____   _____   _____   _____

6. Sometimes, picking a hotel is merely luck. For instance, when she was in budapest, hungary, she stumbled upon the carlton hotel where she ended up staying for four wonderful days.

_____   _____   _____   _____

334 PART 3 Sentence Skills

7. The hotel is located at the base of buda castle and close to a famous suspension bridge that spans the danube river; its proximity allows visitors to walk everywhere they need to go.

   _____ _____ _____ _____

8. Ms. Jones then recommended the premier inn near waterloo station for anyone visiting london because it is incredibly economical and within walking distance of every major site, including parliament.

   _____ _____ _____ _____ _____ _____

9. For people visiting the island of bermuda, ms. jones recommended splurging and staying at the pink beach club and cottages.

   _____ _____ _____ _____
   _____ _____ _____

10. I learned a lot at this year's conference and already have plans to visit budapest during my thanksgiving vacation next year.

    _____ _____

REVIEW TEST 2

On a separate piece of paper, write:

- seven sentences demonstrating the seven main uses of capital letters.
- eight sentences demonstrating the eight other uses of capital letters.

CHAPTER 28

Commas

INTRODUCTORY ACTIVITY

Commas often (though not always) signal a minor break or pause in a sentence. Each of the six pairs of sentences below illustrates one of six main uses of the comma. Read each pair of sentences aloud and place a comma wherever you feel a slight pause occurs. Then choose the rule that applies from the box at the bottom of the page, and write its letter on the line provided.

_____ 1. You can use a credit card write out a check or provide cash.

      The old house was infested with red ants roaches and mice.

_____ 2. To start the car depress the accelerator and turn the ignition key.

      Before you go hiking buy a comfortable pair of shoes.

_____ 3. Leeches creatures that suck human blood are valuable to medical science.

      George Derek who was just arrested was a classmate of mine.

_____ 4. Our professor said the exam would be easy but I thought it was difficult.

      Wind howled through the trees and rain pounded against the window.

_____ 5. Emily asked "Why is it so hard to remember your dreams the next day?"

      "I am so tired after work " Lily said "that I fall asleep right away."

_____ 6. Bert has driven 1500000 accident-free miles in his job as a trucker.

      The Gates Trucking Company of Newark New Jersey gave Bert an award on August 26 2009 for his superior safety record.

---

a.   separate items in a list
b.   separate introductory material from the sentence
c.   separate words that interrupt the sentence
d.   separate complete thoughts in a sentence
e.   separate direct quotations from the rest of the sentence
f.   separate numbers, addresses, and dates in everyday writing

Six Main Uses of the Comma

Commas are used mainly as follows:

- To separate items in a series
- To set off introductory material
- On both sides of words that interrupt the flow of thought in a sentence
- Between two complete thoughts connected by *and, but, for, or, nor, so, yet*
- To set off a direct quotation from the rest of a sentence
- To set off certain everyday material

You may find it helpful to remember that the comma often marks a slight pause, or break, in a sentence. These pauses or breaks occur at the points where the six main comma rules apply. Sentence examples for each of the comma rules are given on the following pages; read these sentences aloud and listen for the minor pauses or breaks that are signaled by commas.

However, you should keep in mind that commas are far more often overused than underused. As a general rule, you should *not* use a comma unless a given comma rule applies or unless a comma is otherwise needed to help a sentence read clearly. A good rule of thumb is that "when in doubt" about whether to use a comma, it is often best to "leave it out."

After reviewing each of the comma rules that follow, you will practice adding commas that are needed and omitting commas that are not needed.

Commas between Items in a Series

Use a comma to separate items in a series.

Magazines, paperback novels, and textbooks crowded the shelves.

Hard-luck Sam needs a loan, a good-paying job, and a close friend.

Pat sat in the doctor's office, checked her watch, and flipped nervously through a magazine.

Mira bit into the ripe, juicy apple.

More and more people entered the crowded, noisy stadium.

> **TIP** A comma is used between two descriptive words in a series only if the word *and* inserted between the words sounds natural. You could say:
>
> Mira bit into the ripe *and* juicy apple.
> More and more people entered the crowded *and* noisy stadium.
>
> But notice in the following sentences that the descriptive words do not sound natural when *and* is inserted between them. In such cases, no comma is used.
>
> The model wore a classy black dress. ("A classy *and* black dress" doesn't sound right, so no comma is used.)
>
> Dr. Van Helsing noticed two tiny puncture marks on the patient's neck. ("Two *and* tiny puncture marks" doesn't sound right, so no comma is used.)

ACTIVITY 1   Commas between Items in a Series

Place commas between items in each series.

1. Mae-Lin tossed her sunglasses a bottle of water and a recent issue of *Every Day with Rachael Ray* into her tote bag.

2. Steve uses the computer to check e-mail play games surf the Internet download music and send instant messages.

3. In the Williams' backyard are an igloo-shaped doghouse several plastic toys trampled flowers and a cracked ceramic gnome.

ACTIVITY 2   Necessary and Unnecessary Commas

For each item, cross out the one comma that is not needed. Add the one comma that is needed between items in a series.

1. I discovered gum wrappers, pennies and a sock hidden, under the seats when I vacuumed my car.

2. Squirrels Canada geese, two white swans, and clouds of mosquitoes, populate Farwell Park.

3. Lewis dribbled twice, spun to his left and lofted his patented hook shot over the outstretched arms, of the Panthers' center.

Commas after Introductory Material

Use a comma to set off introductory material.

Fearlessly, Jessie picked up the slimy slug.

Just to annoy Steve, she let it crawl along her arm.

Although I have a black belt in karate, I decided to go easy on the demented bully who had kicked sand in my face.

Mumbling under her breath, the woman picked over the tomatoes.

> **T I P**   If the introductory material is brief, the comma is sometimes omitted. In the activities here, you should include the comma.

Commas after Introductory Clauses

ACTIVITY 3

Place commas after introductory material.

> **H I N T**   In item 1, the last introductory word is *airport.*

1. Before I left for the airport I turned off my water heater and unplugged my appliances.
2. If you left your backpack at the library you should call Campus Security.
3. Wanting to help others Brian volunteers at the Meals on Wheels program.

More Neccessary and Unnecessary Commas

ACTIVITY 4

For each item, cross out the one comma that is not needed. Add the one comma that is needed after introductory material.

> **H I N T**   In item 1, add a comma to the first sentence and omit the comma in the second.

1. Using metallic cords from her Christmas presents young Ali made several bracelets for herself. After that, she took a long ribbon, and tied a bow around her dog's head.

2. As the bride smiled and strolled past me down the aisle I saw a bead of sweat roll, from her forehead down her cheek. Remembering my own wedding, I knew she wasn't sweating from the heat.

3. When my children were young, I wrote interesting anecdotes about them in a notebook. For example I wrote a note to remind me, that my son once wanted to be a yo-yo maker.

Commas around Words Interrupting the Flow of Thought

Use a comma before and after words that interrupt the flow of thought in a sentence.

The car, cleaned and repaired, is ready to be sold.

Martha, our new neighbor, used to work as a bartender at Rexy's Tavern.

Taking long walks, especially after dark, helps me sort out my thoughts.

Usually you can "hear" words that interrupt the flow of thought in a sentence. However, when you are not sure if certain words are interrupters, remove them from the sentence. If it still makes sense without the words, you know that the words are interrupters and that the information they give is nonessential. Such nonessential information is set off with commas. In the following sentence

Susie Hall, who is my best friend, won a new car in the *Reader's Digest* sweepstakes.

the words *who is my best friend* are extra information, not needed to identify the subject of the sentence, *Susie Hall*. Put commas around such nonessential information. On the other hand, in the sentence

The woman who is my best friend won a new car in the *Reader's Digest* sweepstakes.

the words *who is my best friend* supply essential information that we need to identify the woman. If the words were removed from the sentence, we would no longer know which woman won the sweepstakes. Commas are not used around such essential information.

Here is another example:

The Shining, a novel by Stephen King, is the scariest book I've ever read.

Here the words *a novel by Stephen King* are extra information, not needed to identify the subject of the sentence, *The Shining*. Commas go around such nonessential information. On the other hand, in the sentence

Stephen King's novel *The Shining* is the scariest book I've ever read.

the words *The Shining* are needed to identify the novel because he has written more than one. Commas are not used around such essential information.

Most of the time you will be able to "hear" words that interrupt the flow of thought in a sentence and will not have to think about whether the words are essential or nonessential.

> **TIP**   Some instructors refer to nonessential or extra information that is set off by commas as a *nonrestrictive clause*. Essential information that interrupts the flow of thought is called a *restrictive clause*. No commas are used to set off a restrictive clause.

Commas That Set Off Interrupters   ACTIVITY 5

Add commas to set off interrupting words.

> **HINT** In item 1, the interrupting words are *assisted by no one*.

1. The supply control clerk assisted by no one conducted a quarterly inventory on Tuesday.

2. Jo Ann and Craig who were engaged for a year married last July at a winery in Sonoma.

3. The lawn furniture rusted beyond repair needs to be thrown out.

More Necessary and Unnecessary Commas   ACTIVITY 6

For each item, cross out the one comma that is not needed. Add the comma that is needed to completely set off the interrupting words.

> **HINT** In item 1, the interrupting words are *even the most gigantic*.

1. All trees, even the most gigantic are only 1 percent living tissue; the rest, is deadwood.

2. The city council in a rare fit, of wisdom, established a series of bicycle paths around town.

3. John Adams and Thomas Jefferson, the second and third presidents, of the United States died on the same day in 1826.

4. My aunt, a talkative, woman married a patient man who is a wonderful listener.

Commas between Complete Thoughts Connected by Joining Words

Use a comma between two complete thoughts connected by *and, but, for, or, nor, so,* or *yet* (joining words).

> My parents threatened to throw me out of the house, so I had to stop playing the drums.
>
> The polyester bedsheets had a gorgeous design, but they didn't feel as comfortable as plain cotton sheets.
>
> The teenage girls walked along the hot summer streets, and the teenage boys drove by in their shiny cars.

> **TIP** The comma is optional when the complete thoughts are short:
> Hunter relaxed but Bob kept working.
> The soda was flat so I poured it away.
> We left school early for the furnace had broken down.

372 PART 3 Sentence Skills

Be careful not to use a comma in sentences having *one* subject and a *double* verb. The comma is used only in sentences made up of two complete thoughts (two subjects and two verbs). In the sentence

Mary lay awake that stormy night and listened to the thunder crashing.

there is only one subject (*Mary*) and a double verb (*lay* and *listened*). No comma is needed. Likewise, the sentence

The quarterback kept the ball and plunged across the goal line for a touchdown.

has only one subject (*quarterback*) and a double verb (*kept* and *plunged*); therefore, no comma is needed.

| ACTIVITY 7 | Commas That Connect Complete Thoughts |

Place a comma before a joining word that connects two complete thoughts (two subjects and two verbs). Remember, do *not* place a comma within sentences that have only one subject and a double verb. Mark sentences that are correct with a C

> HINT In item 1, *but* connects two complete thoughts.

1. Christopher Columbus thought he had landed on the continent of India but he actually landed on an island off the coast of North America.

2. George Washington Carver invented different ways to use peanuts and sweet potatoes.

3. Miriam Benjamin was the second black woman to receive a patent for an invention and her invention was a chair with a buzzer that could summon waiters.

4. Admiral Richard E. Byrd was a famous explorer for he took several expeditions to Antarctica in the early twentieth century.

5. The great Russian poet Aleksandr Pushkin disliked the class structure of his country so he wrote about the horrible cruelties of serfdom.

6. Galileo Galilei was an Italian astronomer and physicist and is known as the "father of modern physics."

7. John Hancock was the first person to sign the Declaration of Independence and he was the first governor of Massachusetts.

8. J. R. D. Tata was an important businessman in India and he founded Tata Airlines, which later became Air India.

9. Musical genius Ludwig van Beethoven composed nine symphonies and received a few music lessons from composer Wolfgang Amadeus Mozart.

10. Jonas Salk spent much of his later life trying to develop a vaccine for AIDS for he had had great success in developing the vaccine against polio.

Commas with Direct Quotations

Use a comma or commas to set off a direct quotation from the rest of a sentence.

"Please take a number," said the deli clerk.

Chris told Sophia, "I've just signed up for a course on Web-page design."

"Those who sling mud," a famous politician once said, "usually lose ground."

"Reading this book," complained Stan, "is about as interesting as watching paint dry."

> TIP   Commas and periods at the end of a quotation go inside quotation marks. See also page 356.

Setting Off Quotations with Commas   ACTIVITY 8

In each sentence, add the one or more commas needed to set off the quoted material.

> HINT   In item 1, add a comma after the quoted material.

1. "Think before you speak" said my dad.
2. "A child miseducated" said John F. Kennedy "is a child lost."
3. "Before you leave the building" muttered the night patrol officer "be sure to sign out."

More Necessary and Unnecessary Commas   ACTIVITY 9

In each item, cross out the one comma that is not needed to set off a quotation. Add the comma(s) needed to set off a quotation from the rest of the sentence.

> HINT   In item 1, add a comma before the quoted material.

1. "If you're looking for a career change," read the poster, in the subway station "consider the US Armed Forces."
2. "Your arms look fine" said the swimming instructor, "but you keep forgetting, to kick."
3. "Did you really think" the judge asked, the defendant, "you could kill both your parents and then ask for mercy because you're an orphan?"

374   PART 3   Sentence Skills

Commas with Everyday Material

Use commas to set off certain everyday material, as shown in the following sections.

Persons Spoken to

I think, Bella, that you should go to bed.

Please turn down the stereo, Mark.

Please, sir, can you spare a dollar?

Dates

Our house was burglarized on June 28, 2013, and two weeks later on July 11, 2013.

Addresses

Robyn's sister lives at 342 Red Oak Drive, Los Angeles, California 90057. She is moving to Manchester, Vermont, after her divorce.

> TIP   No comma is used before a zip code.

Openings and Closings of Letters

Dear Marilyn,	Sincerely,
Dear John,	Truly yours,

In formal letters, a colon is used after the opening:

Dear Sir:

Dear Madam:

Numbers

Government officials estimate that Americans spend about 785,000,000 hours a year filling out federal forms.

ACTIVITY 10 | **Adding Commas**

Place commas where needed.

 HINT   Two commas are needed in item 1.

1. Excuse me madam but your scarf is in my soup.
2. Before age eighteen, the average child spends 6000 hours in school and 15000 hours watching television.

3. The famous ocean liner *Titanic* sank in the Atlantic Ocean on April 151912.

4. Teresa

   What do you think of this psychology lecture? Will you meet me for lunch after class? I'll treat. Text me your answer right away.

   Love
Jeff

5. The zoo in Washington D.C. purchases 50000 pounds of meat; 6500 loaves of bread; 114000 live crickets; and other foods for its animals each year.

Unnecessary Use of Commas

Remember that if no clear rule applies for using a comma, it is usually better not to use one. As stated previously, "When in doubt, leave it out." Following are some typical examples of unnecessary commas.

Incorrect

Sharon told me, that my socks were different colors.

(A comma is not used before *that* unless the flow of thought is interrupted.)

The union negotiations, dragged on for three days.

(Do not use a comma between a simple subject and verb.)

I waxed all the furniture, and cleaned the windows.

(Use a comma before *and* only with more than two items in a series or when *and* joins two complete thoughts.)

Liz carried, the baby into the house.

(Do not use a comma between a verb and its object.)

I had a clear view, of the entire robbery.

Do not use a comma before a prepositional phrase.)

Eliminating Unnecessary Commas	ACTIVITY 11

Cross out commas that do not belong. Some commas are correct. Do not add any commas.

1. We grew a pumpkin last year, that weighed over one hundred pounds.

2. Anyone with a failing grade, must meet with the instructor during office hours.

3. Last weekend a grizzly bear attacked a hiker, who got too close to its cubs.

4. After watching my form, on the high-diving board, Mr. Riley, my instructor, asked me if I had insurance.

5. Rosa flew first to Los Angeles, and then she went to visit her parents, in Mexico City.

6. The tall muscular man wearing the dark sunglasses, is a professional wrestler.

7. Onions, radishes, and potatoes, seem to grow better in cooler climates.

8. Whenever Vincent is in Las Vegas, you can find him at the blackjack table, or the roulette wheel.

9. While I watched in disbelief, my car rolled down the hill, and through the front window of a Chinese restaurant.

10. The question, sir, is not, whether you committed the crime, but, when you committed the crime.

ACTIVITY 12   Editing and Rewriting

Working with a partner, read carefully the short paragraph below and cross out the five misplaced commas. Then insert the ten additional commas needed. Feel free to discuss the rewrite quietly with your partner and refer back to the chapter when necessary.

Dear Olivia,

On Tuesday, May 5 2009 my husband, and I were unable to sleep because of the loud music coming from your apartment. When I first heard the music I didn't say anything to you because it was still early. But the music, along with loud, laughter and talking, continued until around four o'clock in the morning. At midnight, my husband went into the hallway to see what was happening and he ran into one of your guests. The man who seemed very drunk stared at him, and said "Go back to bed, old man." The next morning, we found beer cans pizza boxes, and cigarette butts, piled outside our door. This is unacceptable. We have written this letter to you as a warning. The next time something like this happens we will call the police, and the building manager. We don't want to cause trouble with you but we will not tolerate another incident like what happened that night.

Sincerely,

Rose Connelly

Creating Sentences

Working with a partner, write sentences that use commas as directed.

1. Write a sentence mentioning three items you want to get the next time you go to the store.

   _____

   _____

2. Write two sentences describing how you relax after getting home from school or work. Start the first sentence with *After* or *When*. Start the second sentence with *Next*.

   _____

   _____

3. Write a sentence that tells something about your favorite movie, book, television show, or song. Use the words *which is my favorite movie* (or *book, television show*, or *song*) after the name of the movie, book, television show, or song.

   _____

   _____

4. Write two complete thoughts about a person you know. The first thought should mention something that you like about the person. The second thought should mention something you don't like. Join the two thoughts with *but*. Do not use the name of a classmate.

   _____

   _____

5. Invent a line that Lola might say to Tony. Use the words *Lola said* in the sentence. Then include Tony's reply, using the words *Tony responded*.

   _____

   _____

6. Write a sentence about an important event in your life. Include the day, month, and year of the event.

   _____

   _____

378   PART 3   Sentence Skills

REFLECTIVE ACTIVITY

1. Look at the letter that you revised on page 376. Explain how adding commas has affected the paragraph.
2. What would writing be like without the comma? How do commas help writing?
3. What is the most difficult comma rule for you to remember and apply? Explain, giving an example.

REVIEW TEST 1

Academic

For each sentence, do three things: (1) Cross out the one comma that is not needed; (2) add the one comma that is needed; and (3) in the space provided, write the letter of the rule that applies for each comma you added.

a. Between items in a series   d. Between complete thoughts

b. After introductory material   e. With direct quotations

c. Around interrupters

_____ 1. William I, known as William the Conqueror was England's first, king in 1066.

_____ 2. Richard Coeur de Lion was often called Richard the Lionheart and he was the king, from 1189 to 1199.

_____ 3. Richard III was the king for only two years, from 1483 until 1485 because of the bad, press he received.

_____ 4. Henry VIII married six different women: Catherine of Aragon, Anne Boleyn Jane Seymour, Anne of Cleves, Kathryn Howard, and Katherine, Parr.

_____ 5. Reigning for only fourteen days until her throne was seized Lady Jane Grey became Queen Jane, in 1553 and was later beheaded.

_____ 6. After she seized the throne, from Mary I Elizabeth I reigned from 1558 to 1603.

_____ 7. George III (1738–1820) wrote "I can never suppose this country so far lost to all ideas of self-importance as to be willing to grant America, independence."

_____ 8. Queen Victoria reigned from 1837 until 1901 but she spent the last forty years of her life, mourning the death of her husband, Albert.

_____ 9. George VI (1936 until 1952), was earnest when he said "The highest of distinctions is service to others."

_____ 10. Queen Elizabeth II was crowned, in 1952 and has four children: Prince Charles Princess Anne, Prince Andrew, and Prince Edward.

REVIEW TEST 2

Insert commas where needed. One sentence does not need commas. Mark it with a C.

1. Some people believe that television can be addictive but I think they're wrong.

2. While there are people who turn on their TVs upon waking up in the morning I don't do that.

3. I turn on my TV only upon sitting down for breakfast and then I watch the *Today Show*.

4. I don't need to watch game shows soap operas and situation comedies to get through the day.

5. Instead I watch all these programs simply because I enjoy them.

6. I also keep the TV turned on all evening because thanks to cable and On Demand there is always something decent to watch.

7. If I did not have good viewing choices I would flick off the TV without hesitation.

8. Lots of people switch channels rapidly to preview what is on.

9. I on the other hand turn immediately to the channel I know I want.

10. In other words I am not addicted; I am a selective viewer who just happens to select a lot of shows.

REVIEW TEST 3

On a separate piece of paper, write six sentences, with each sentence demonstrating one of the six main comma rules.